Abstractions

Leou

Abstractions 5

ISBN : 9781086791815

nicolaslehoux.com

Abstractions

tome5

art
Leou

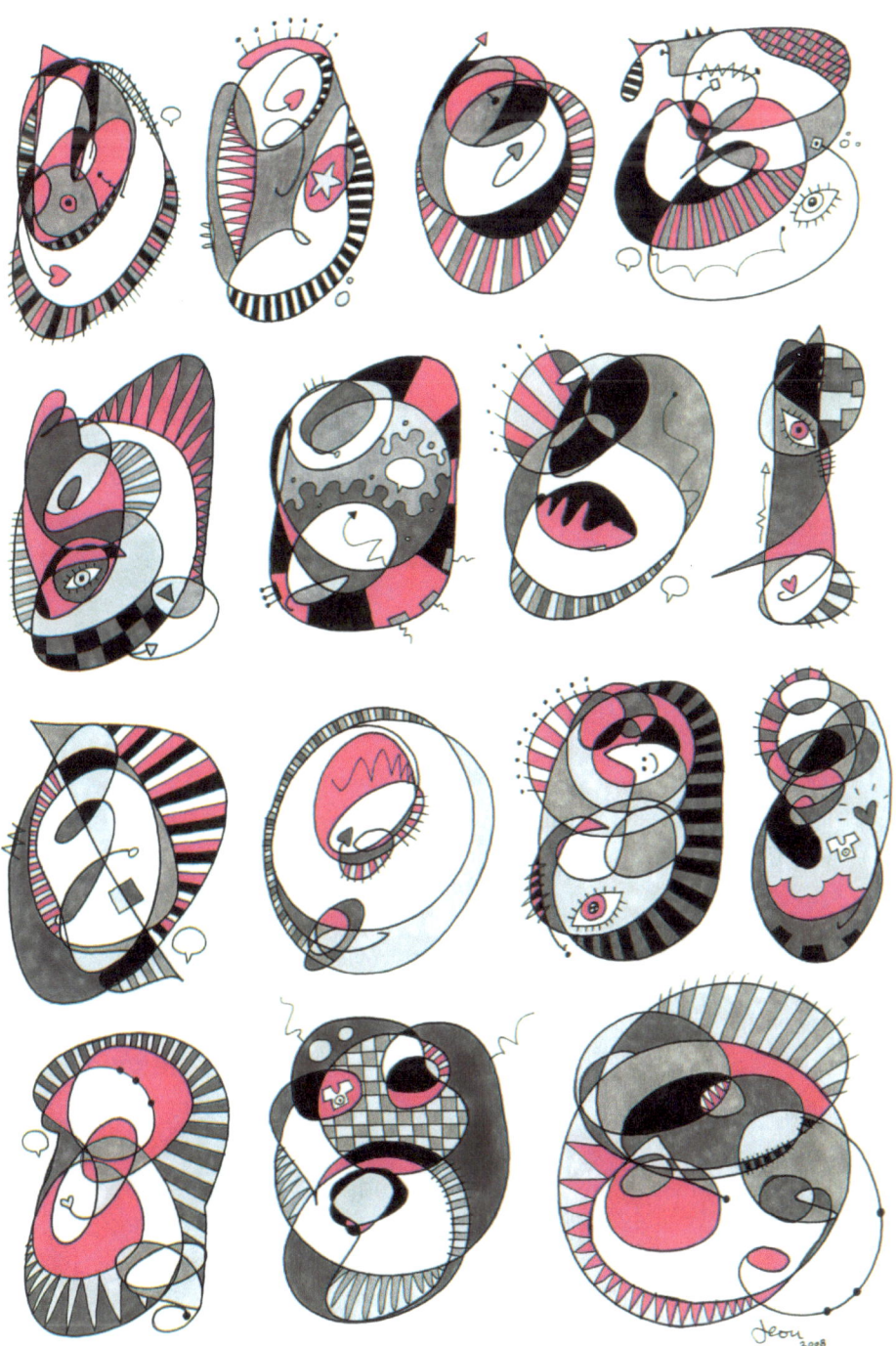

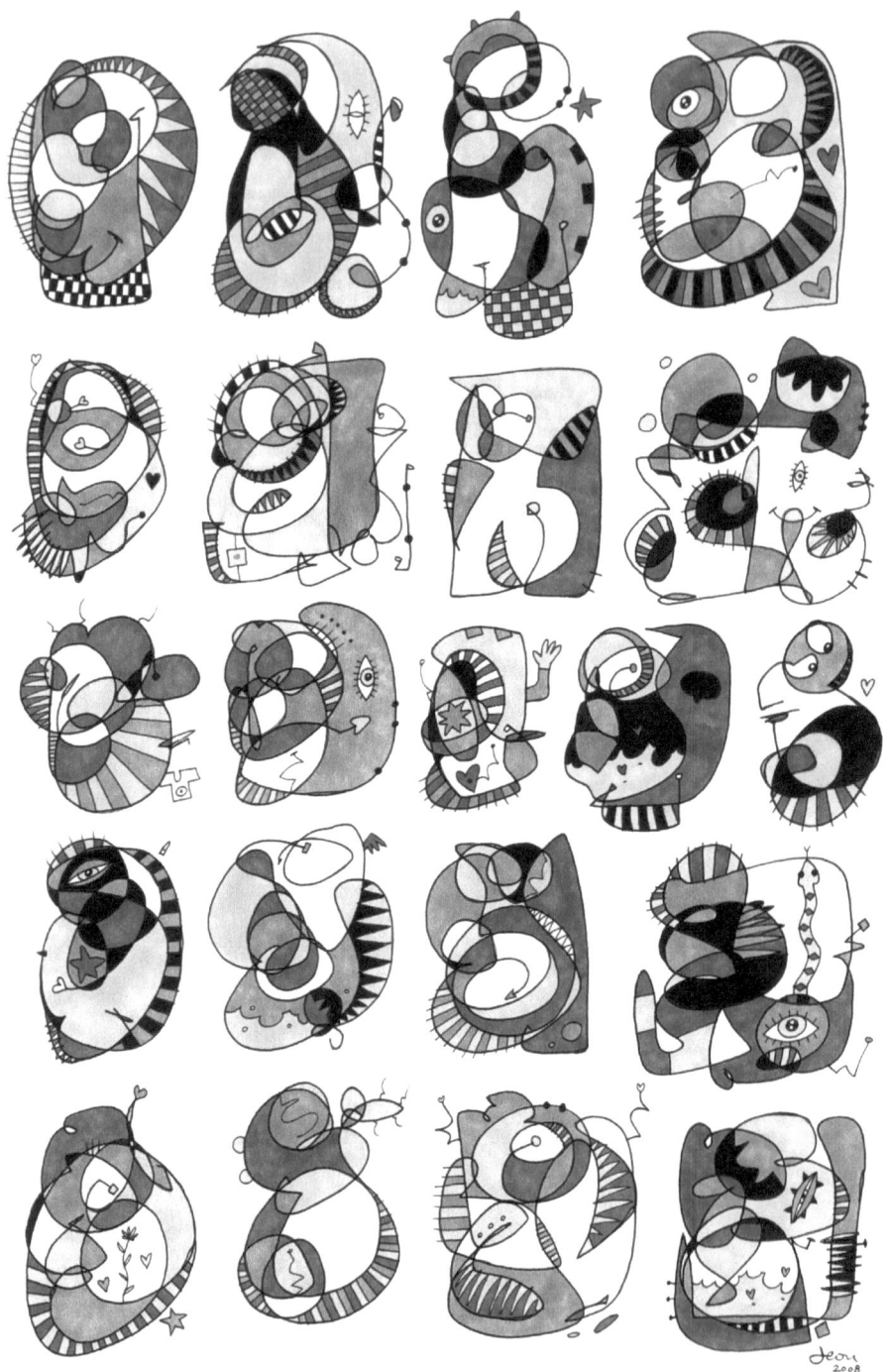

8

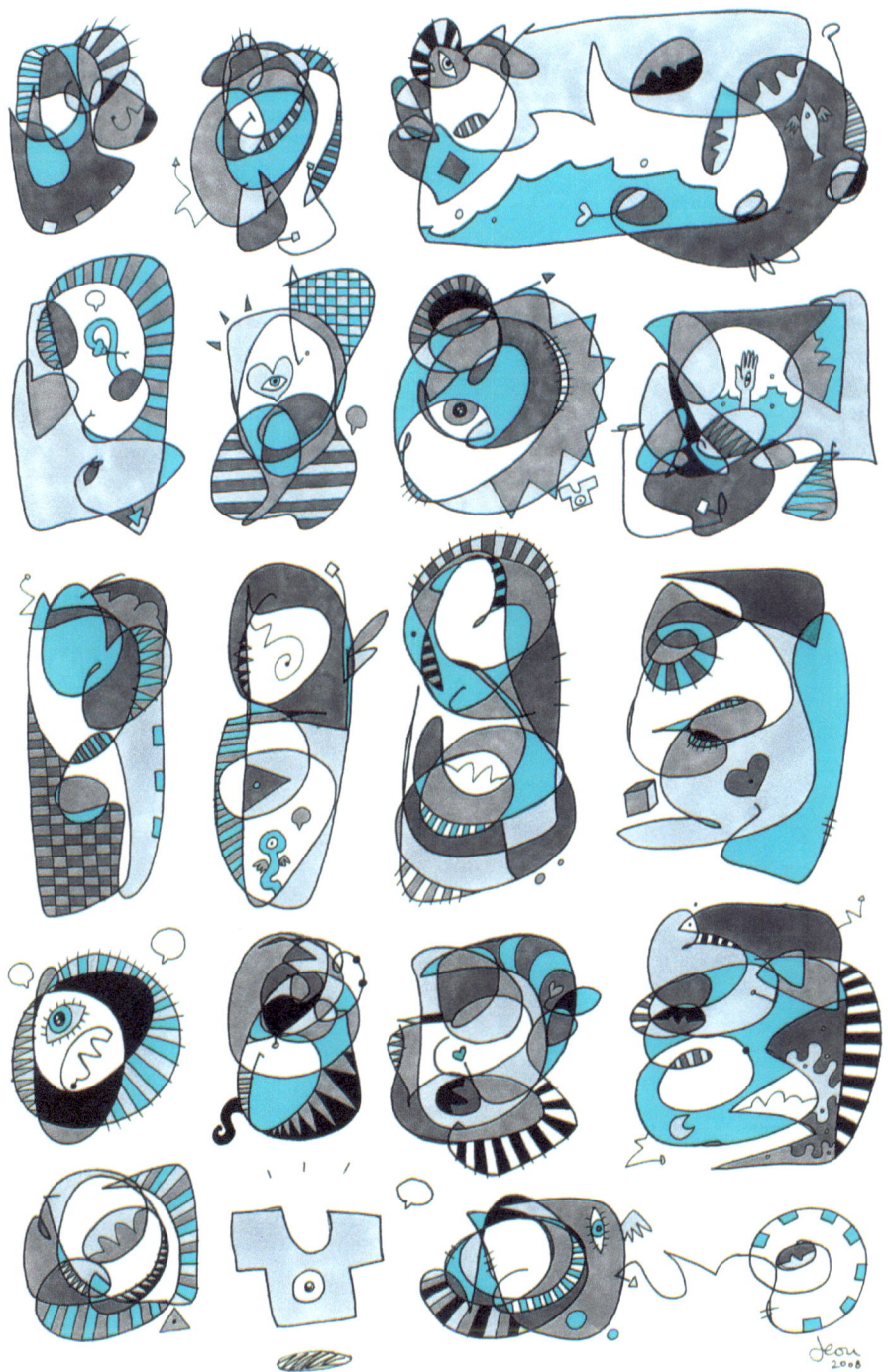

9

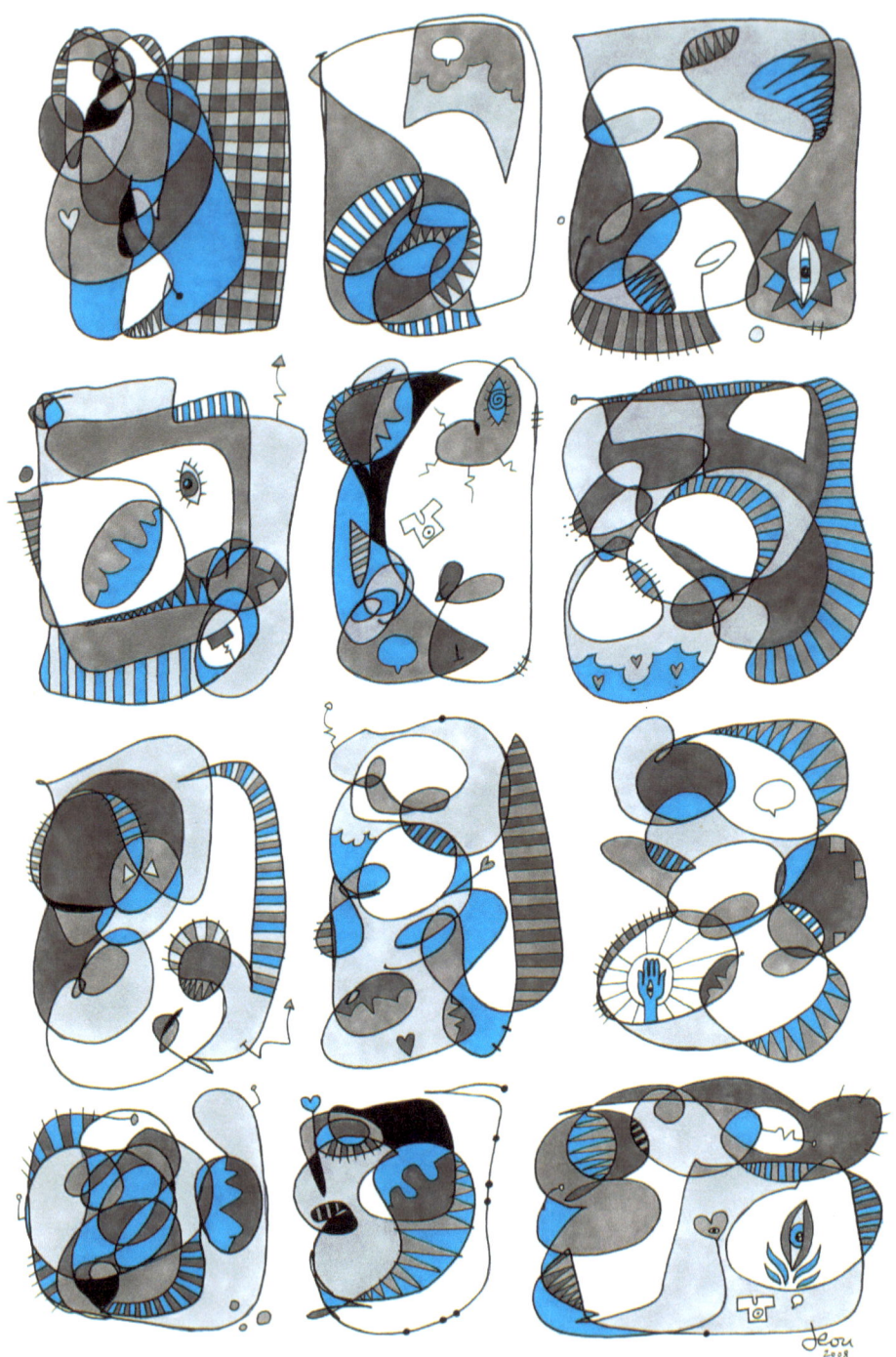

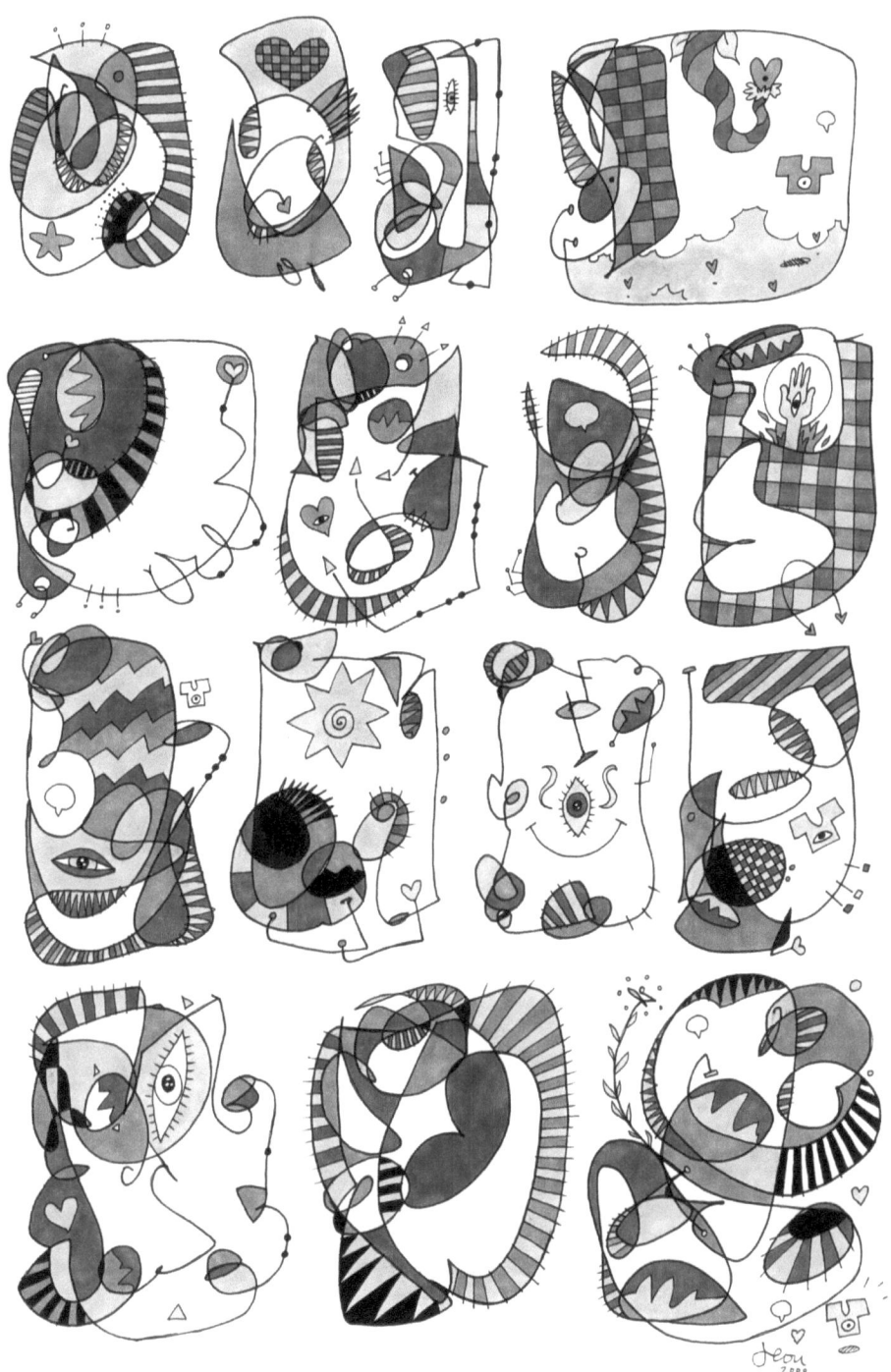

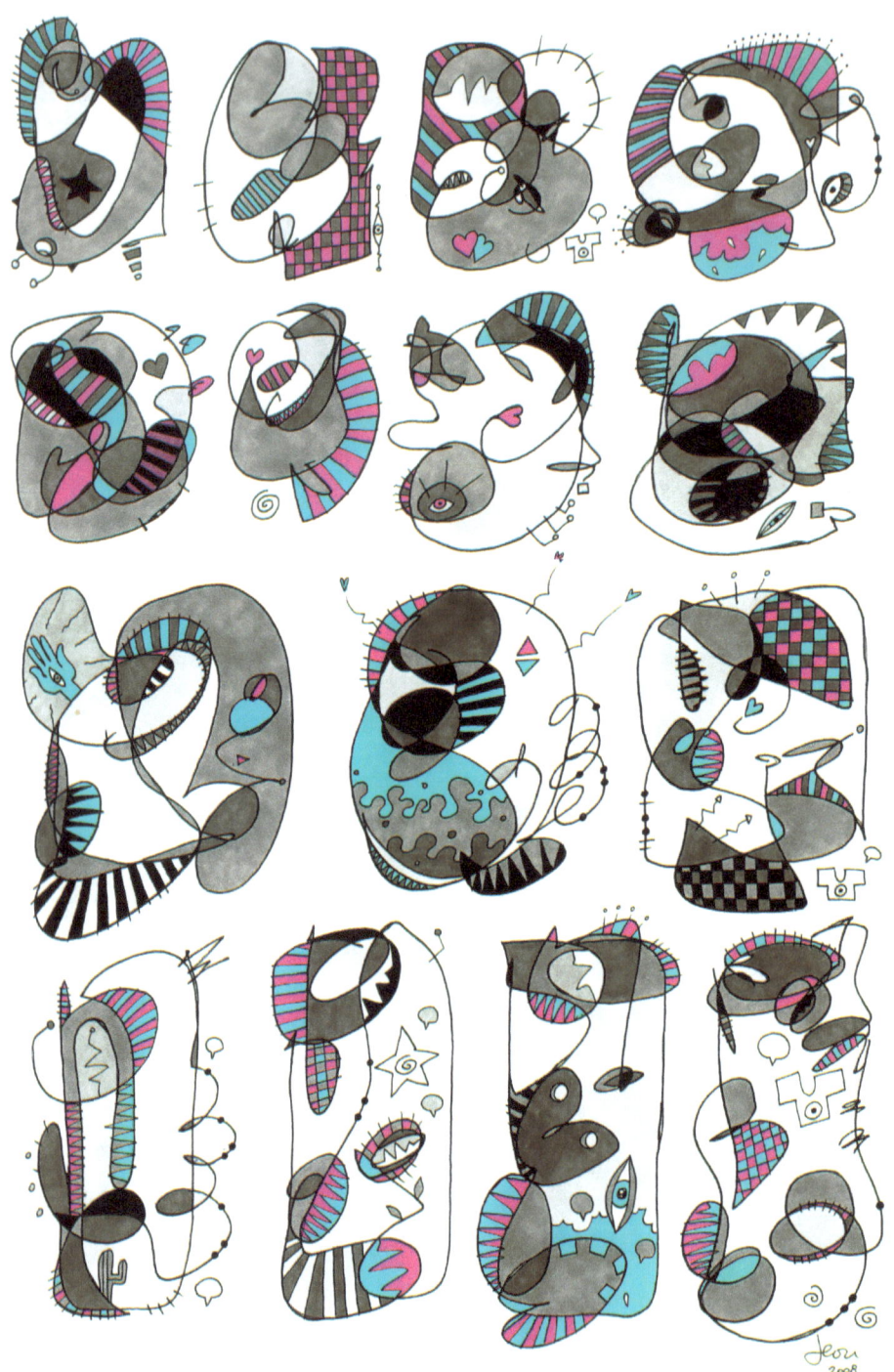

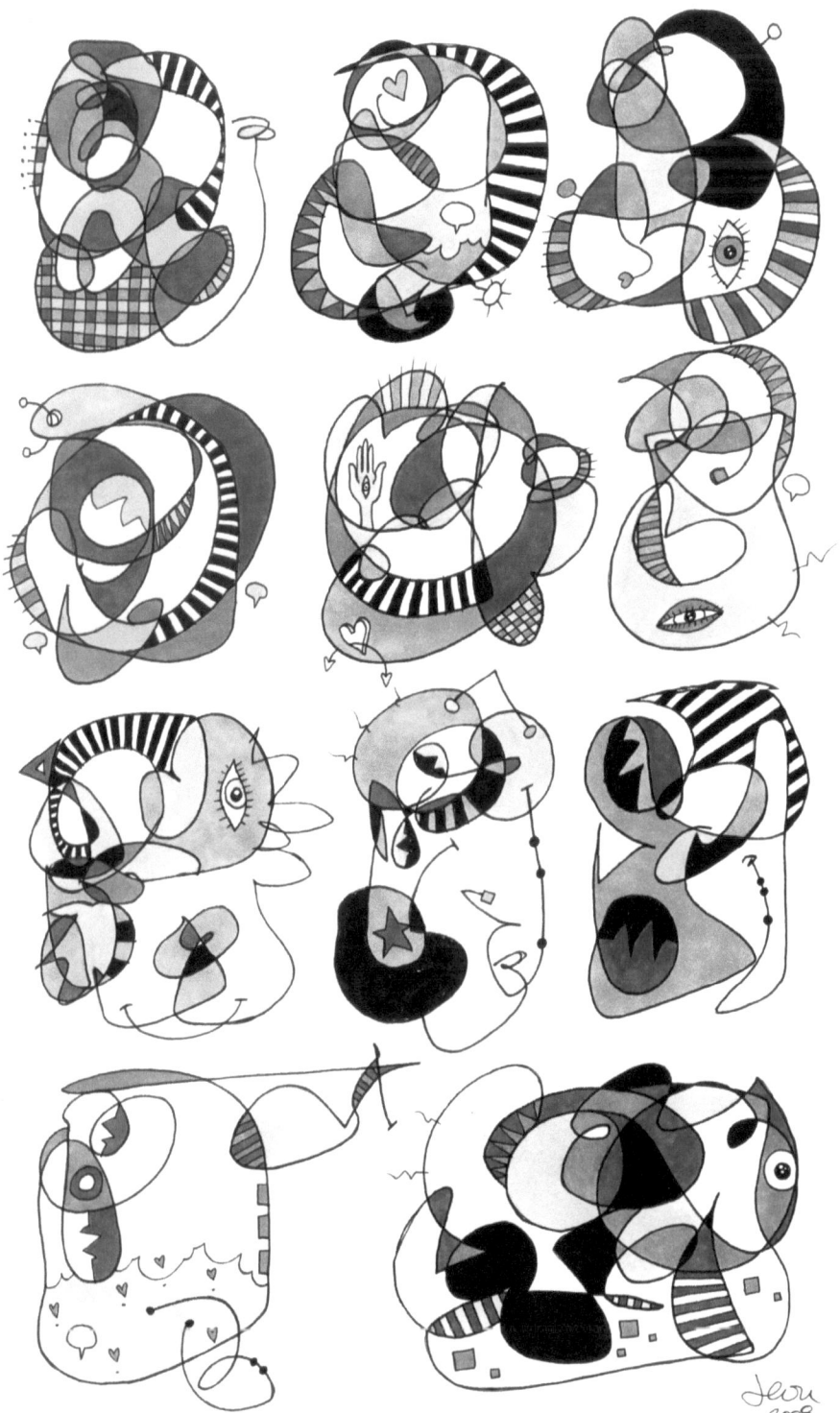

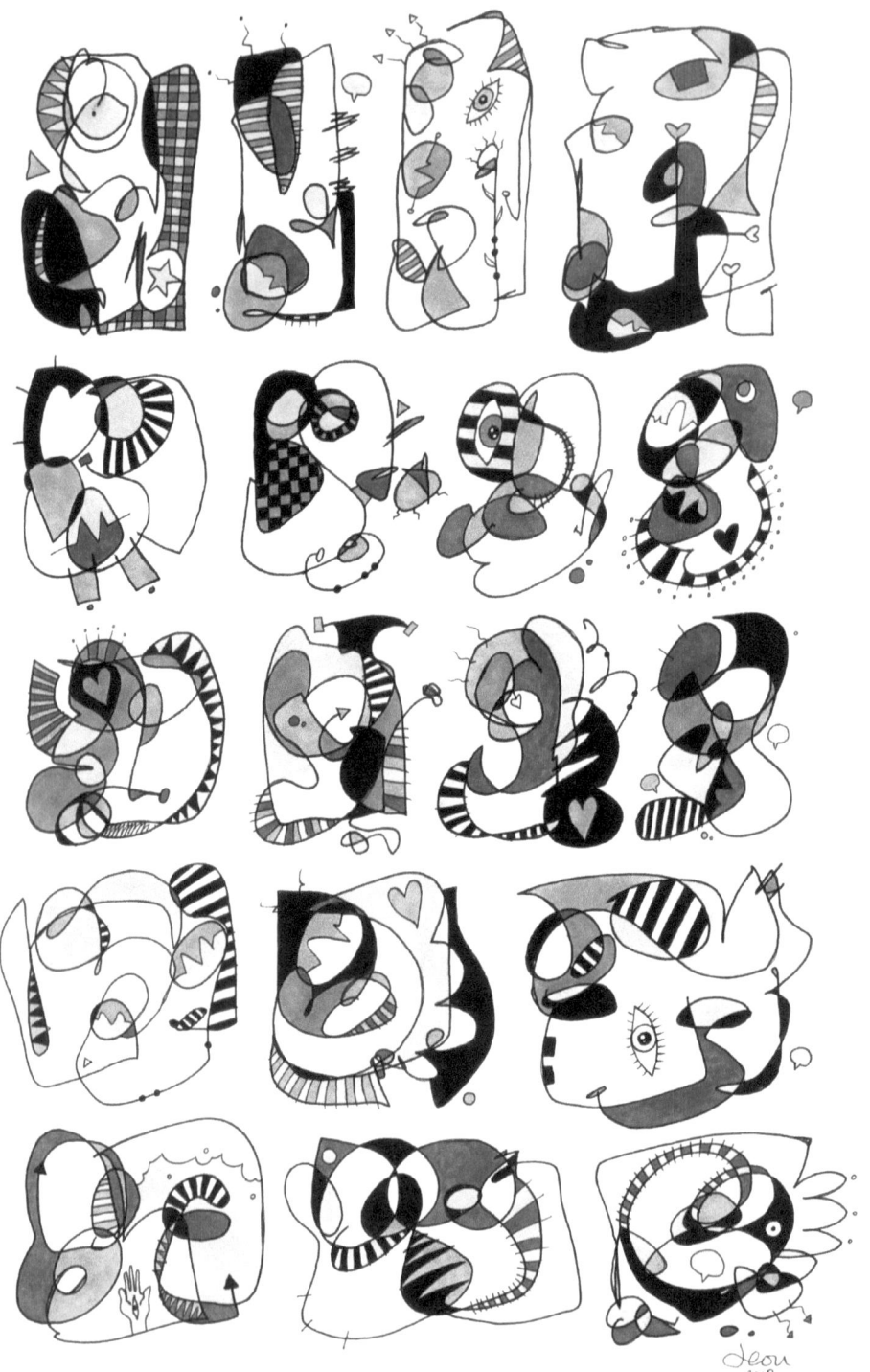

14

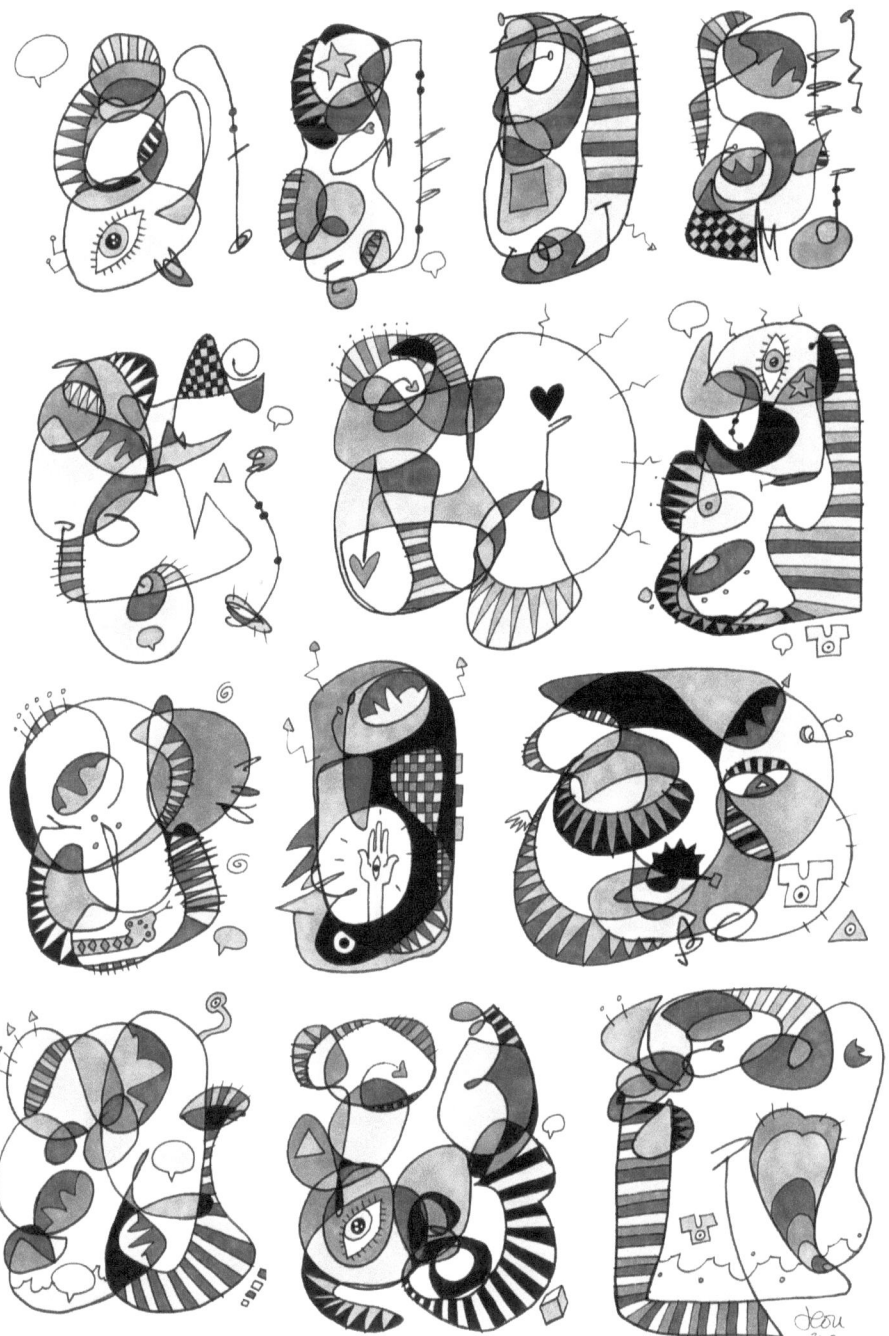

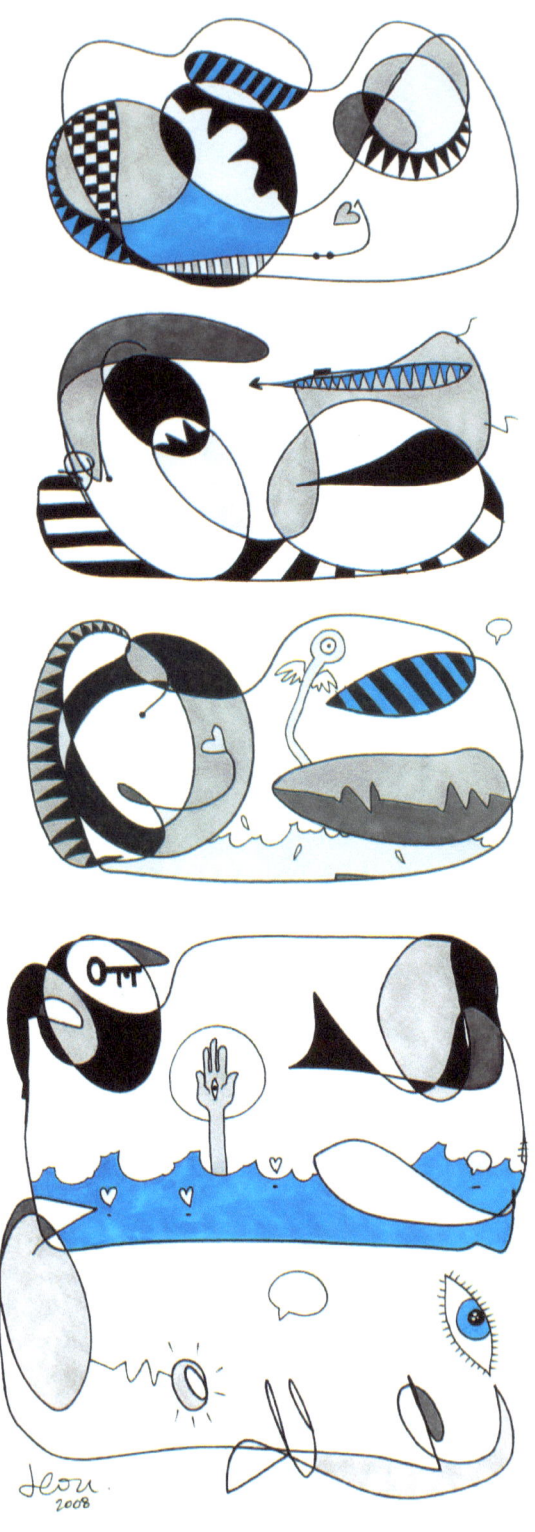

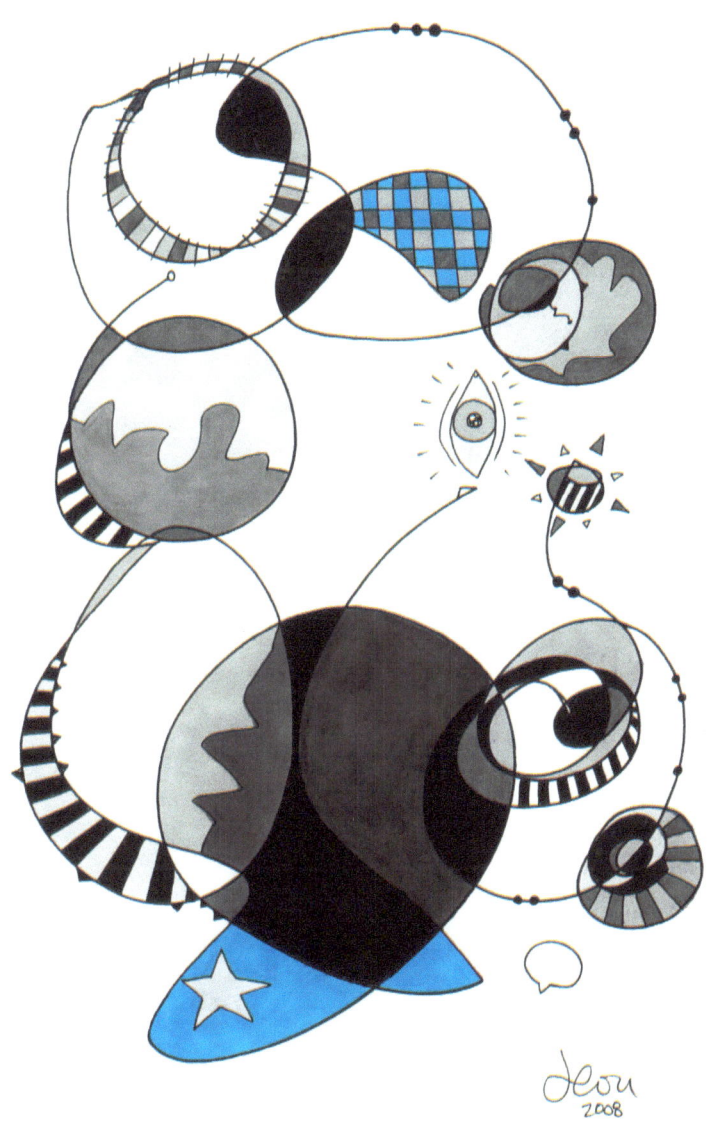

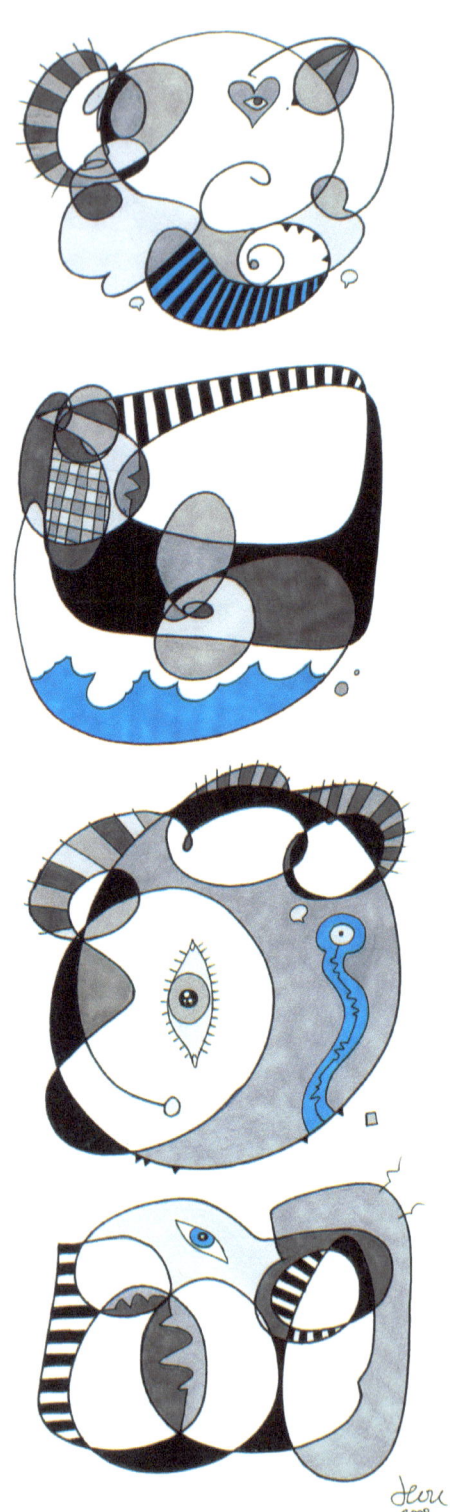

18

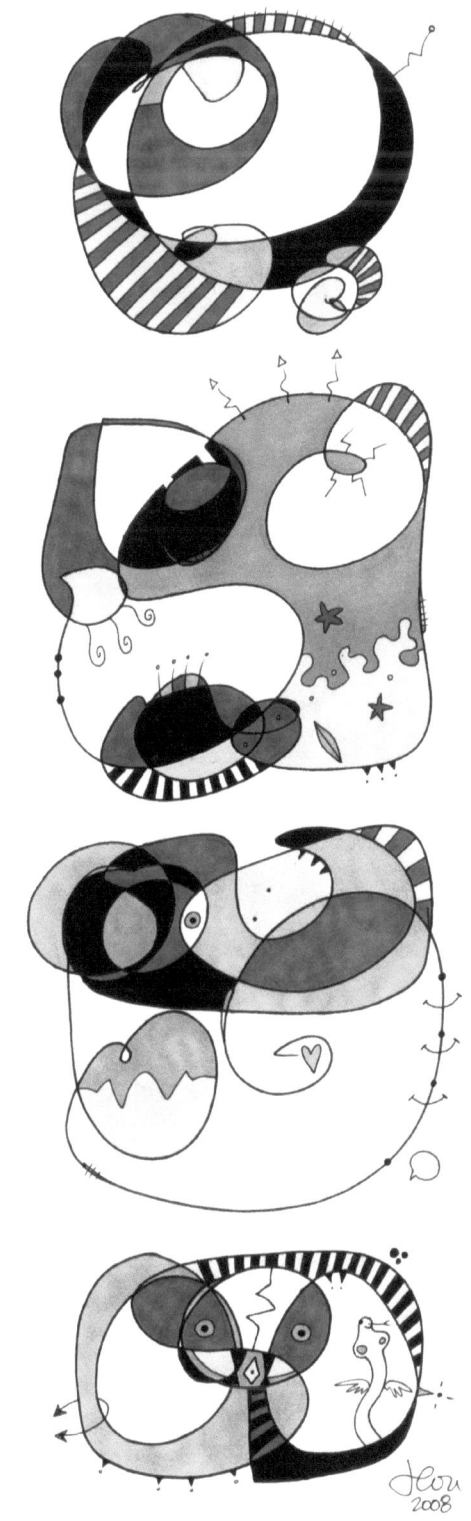

19

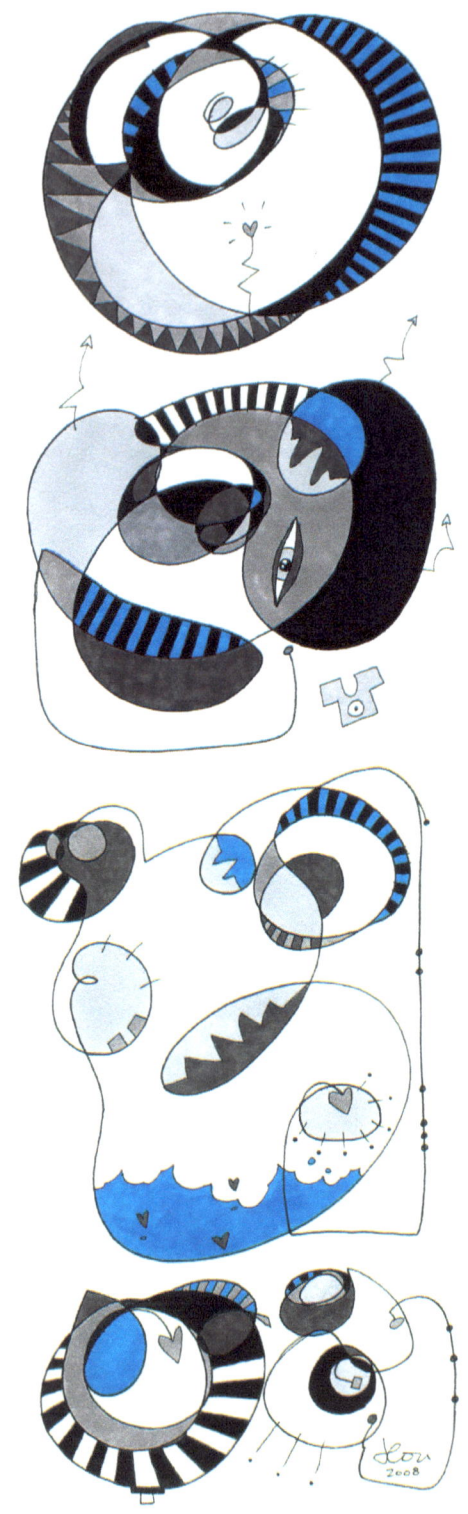

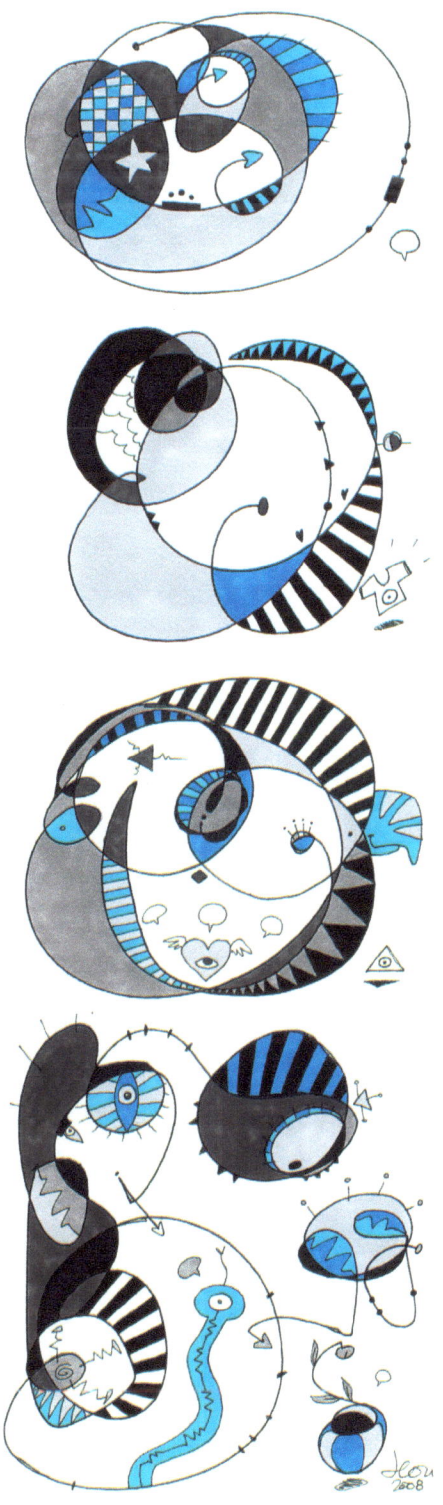

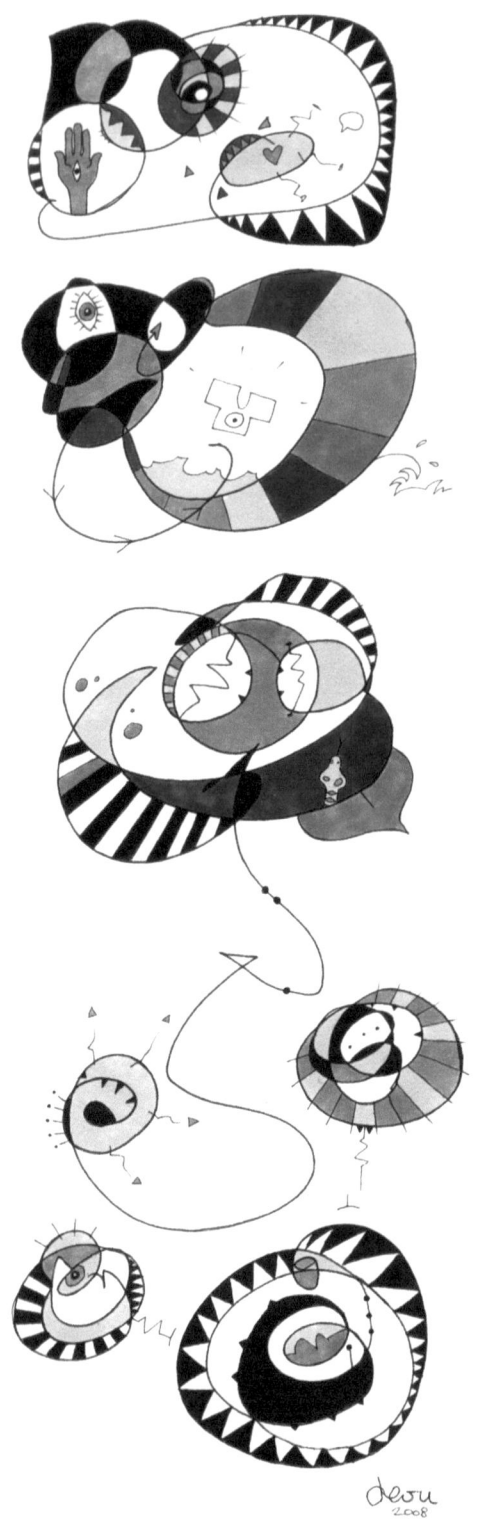

22

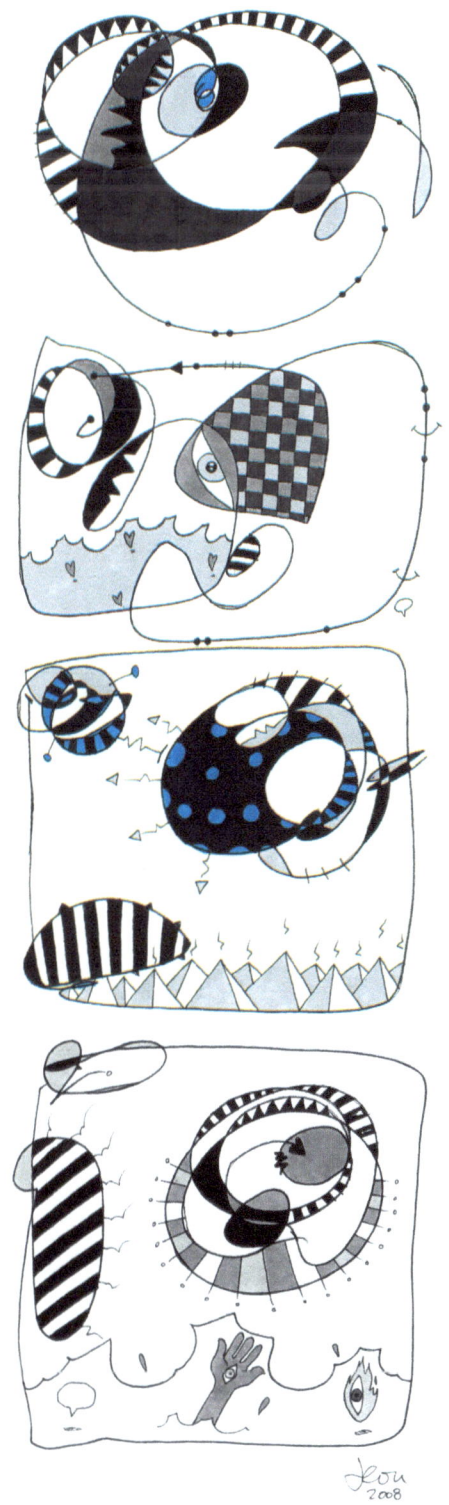

23

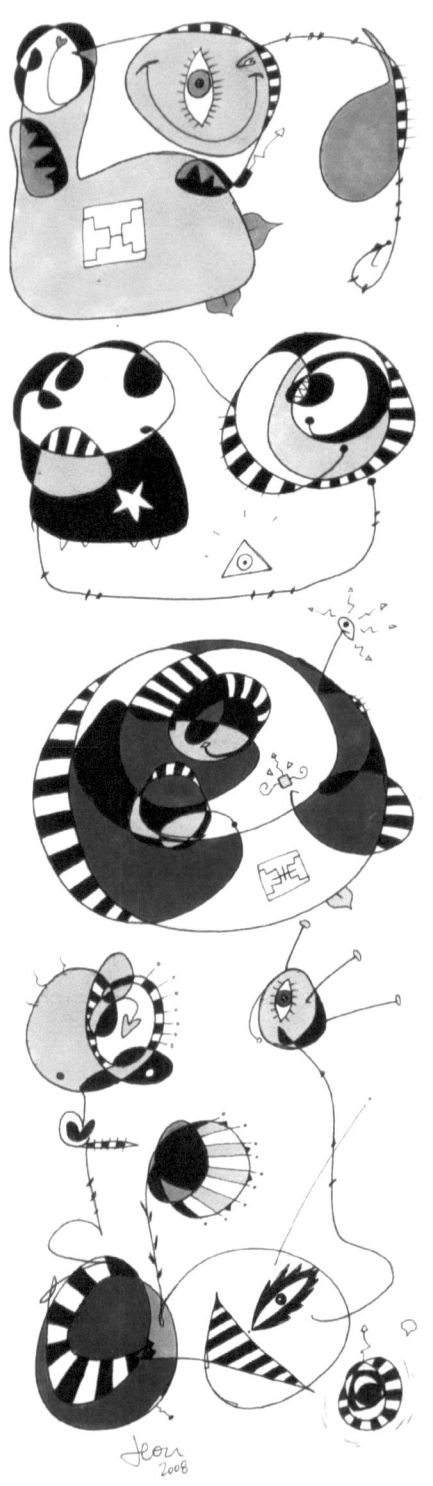

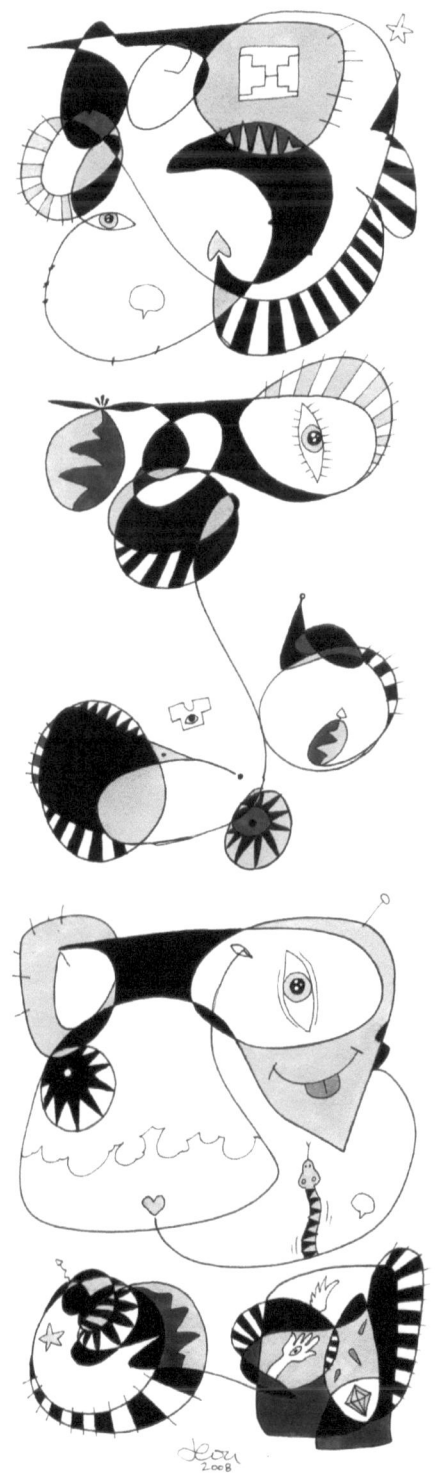

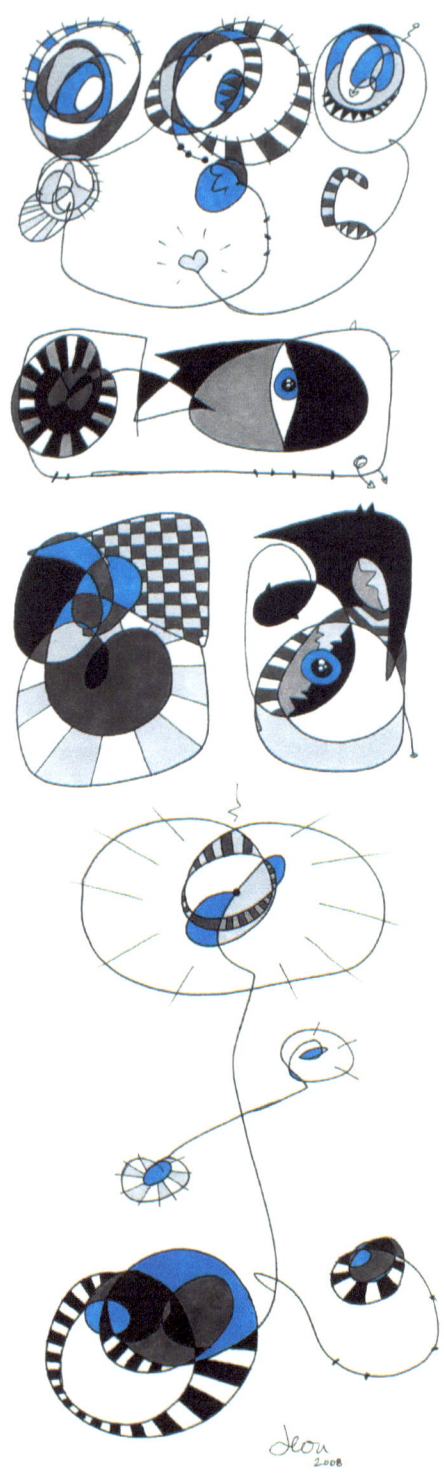

26

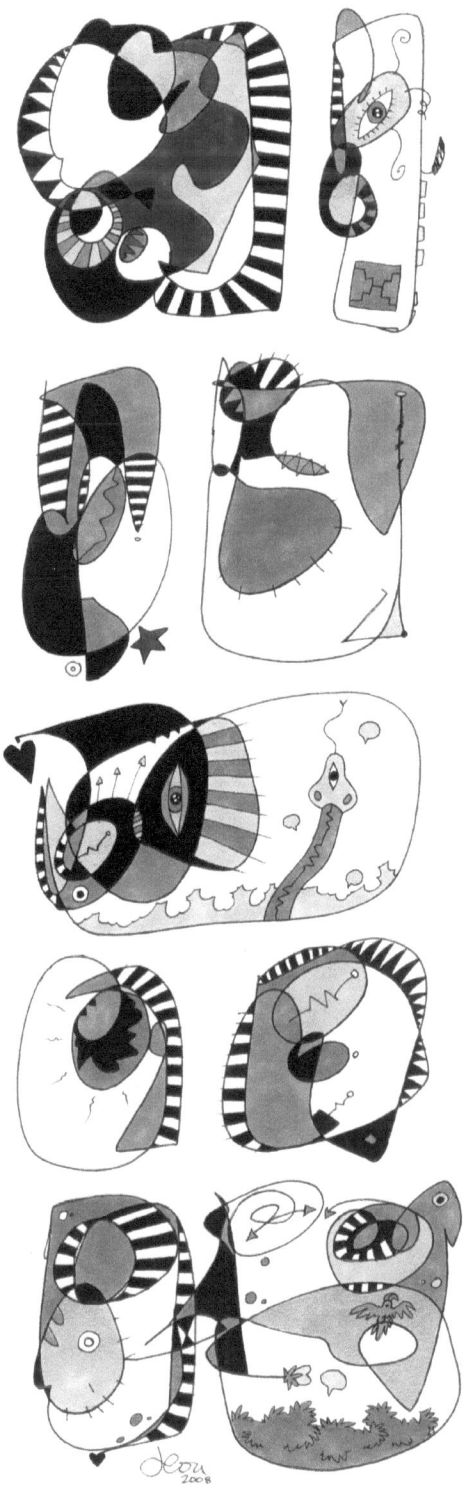

27

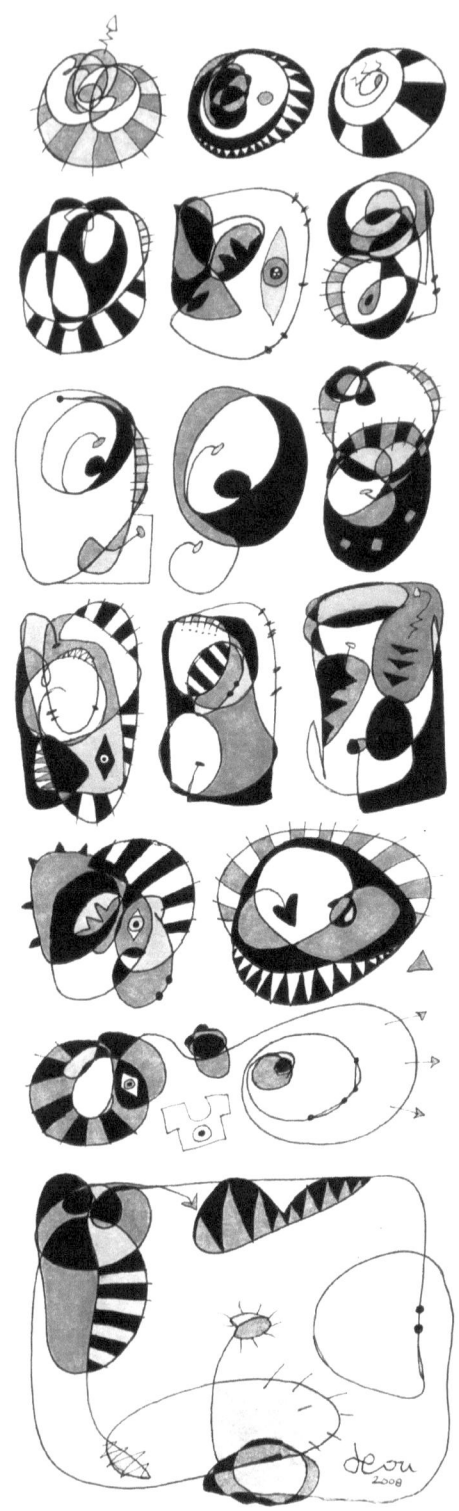

28

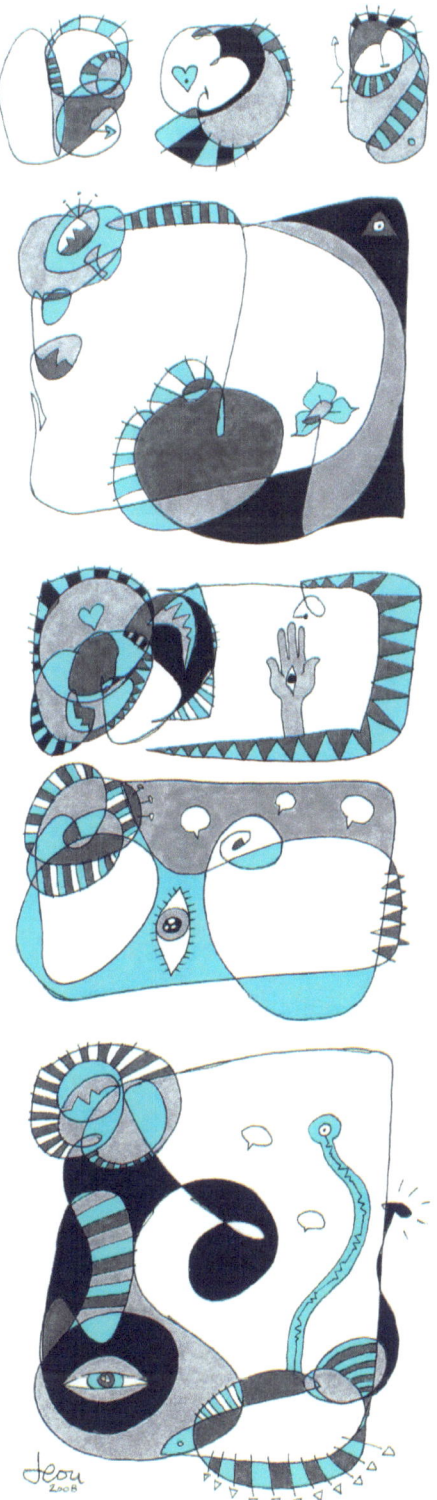

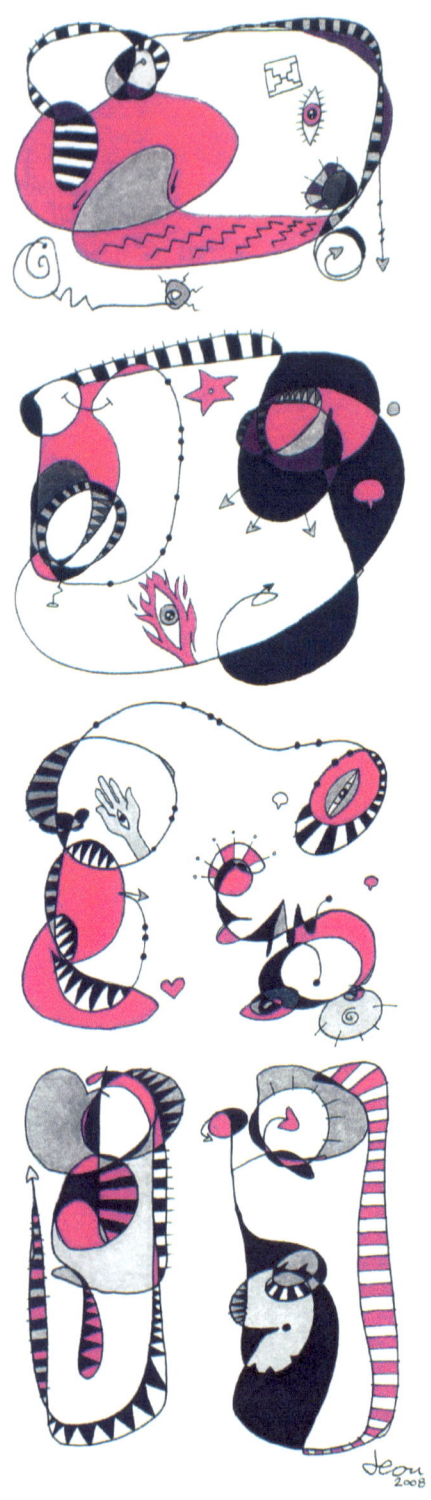

30

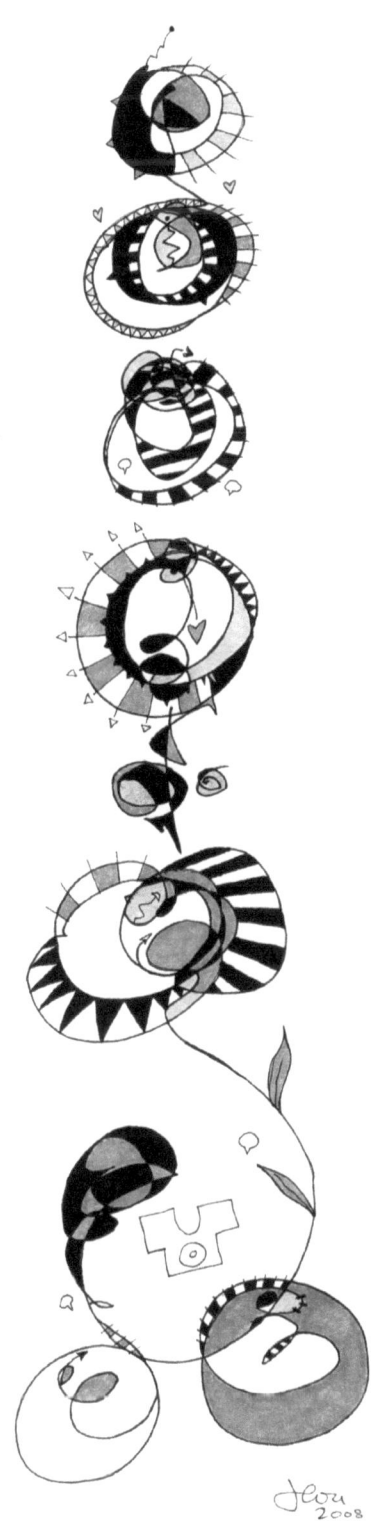

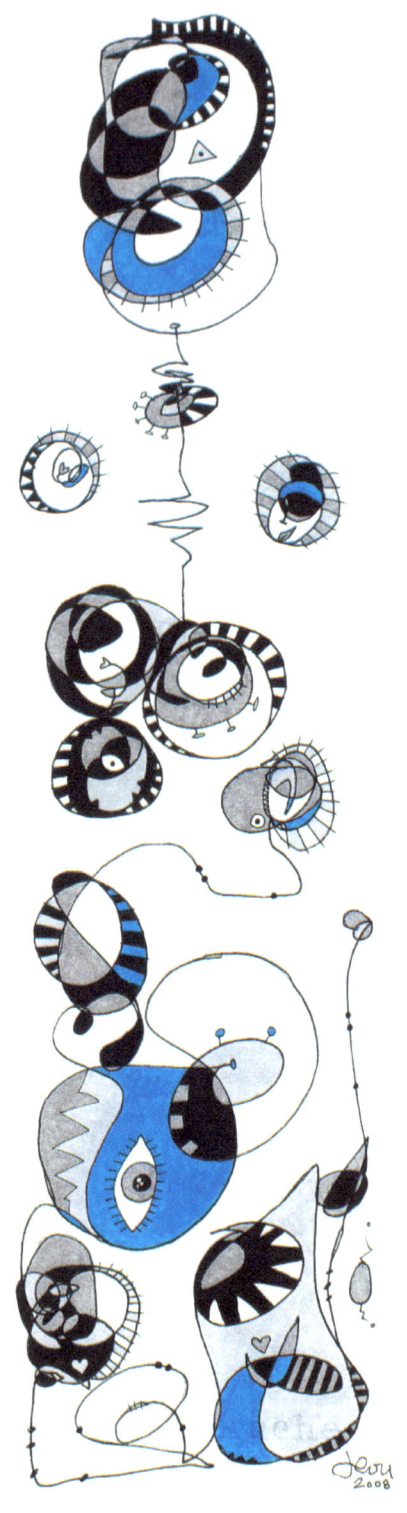

32

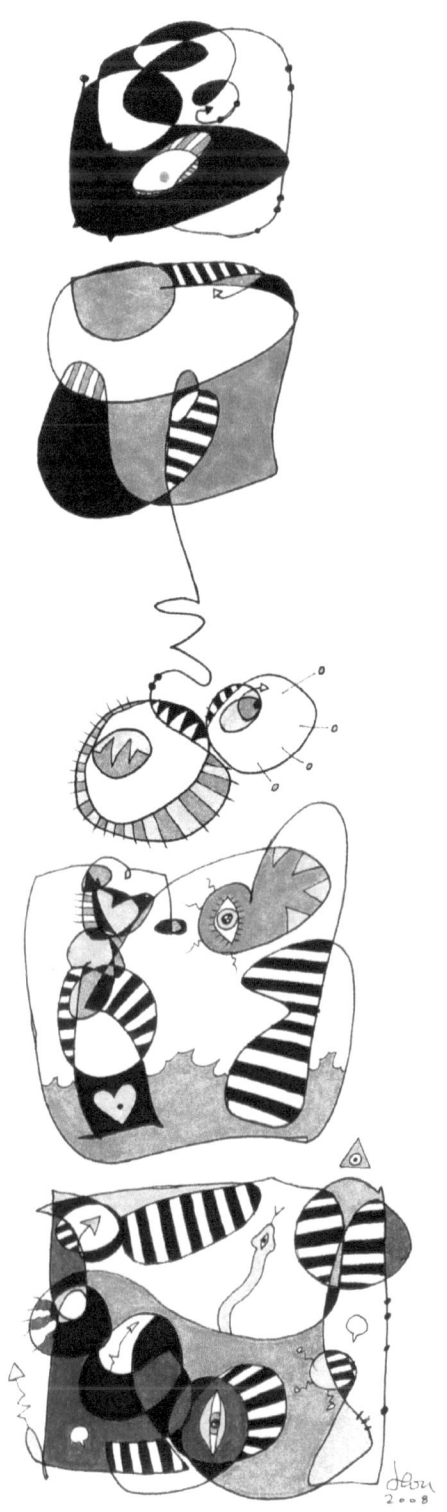

33

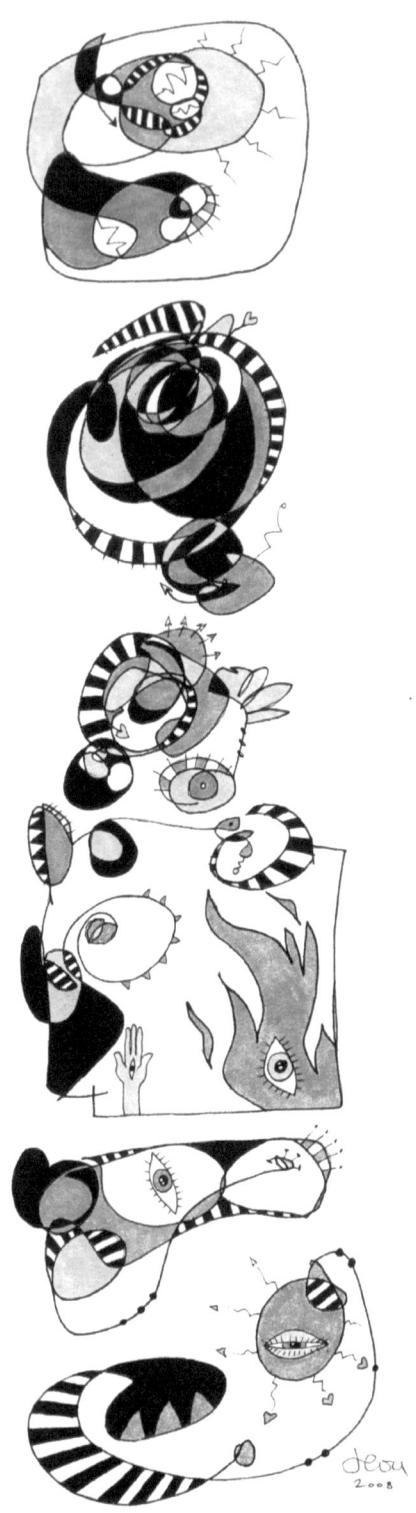

34

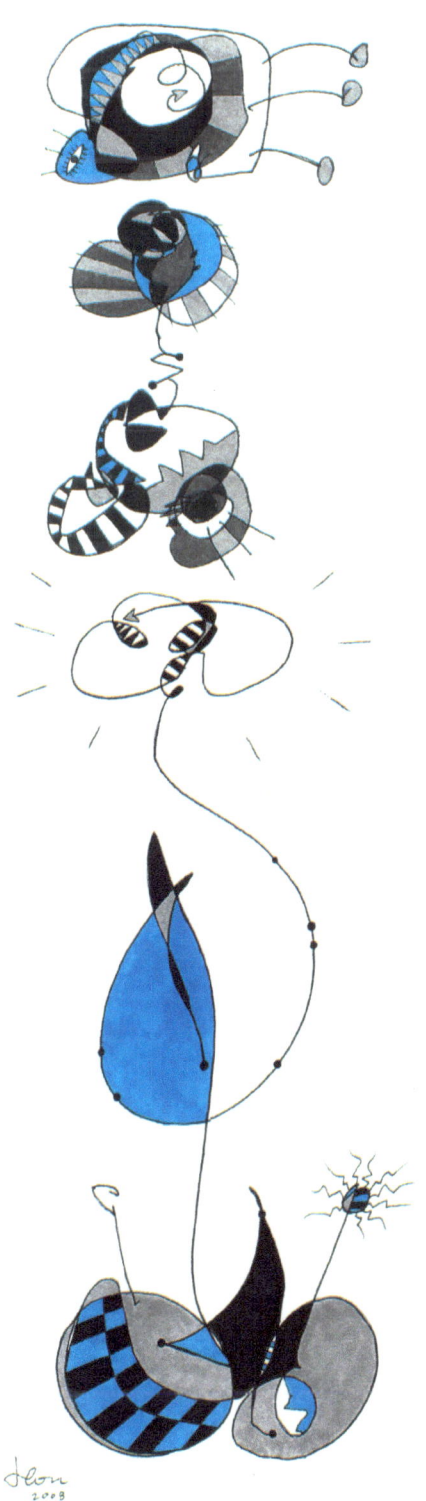

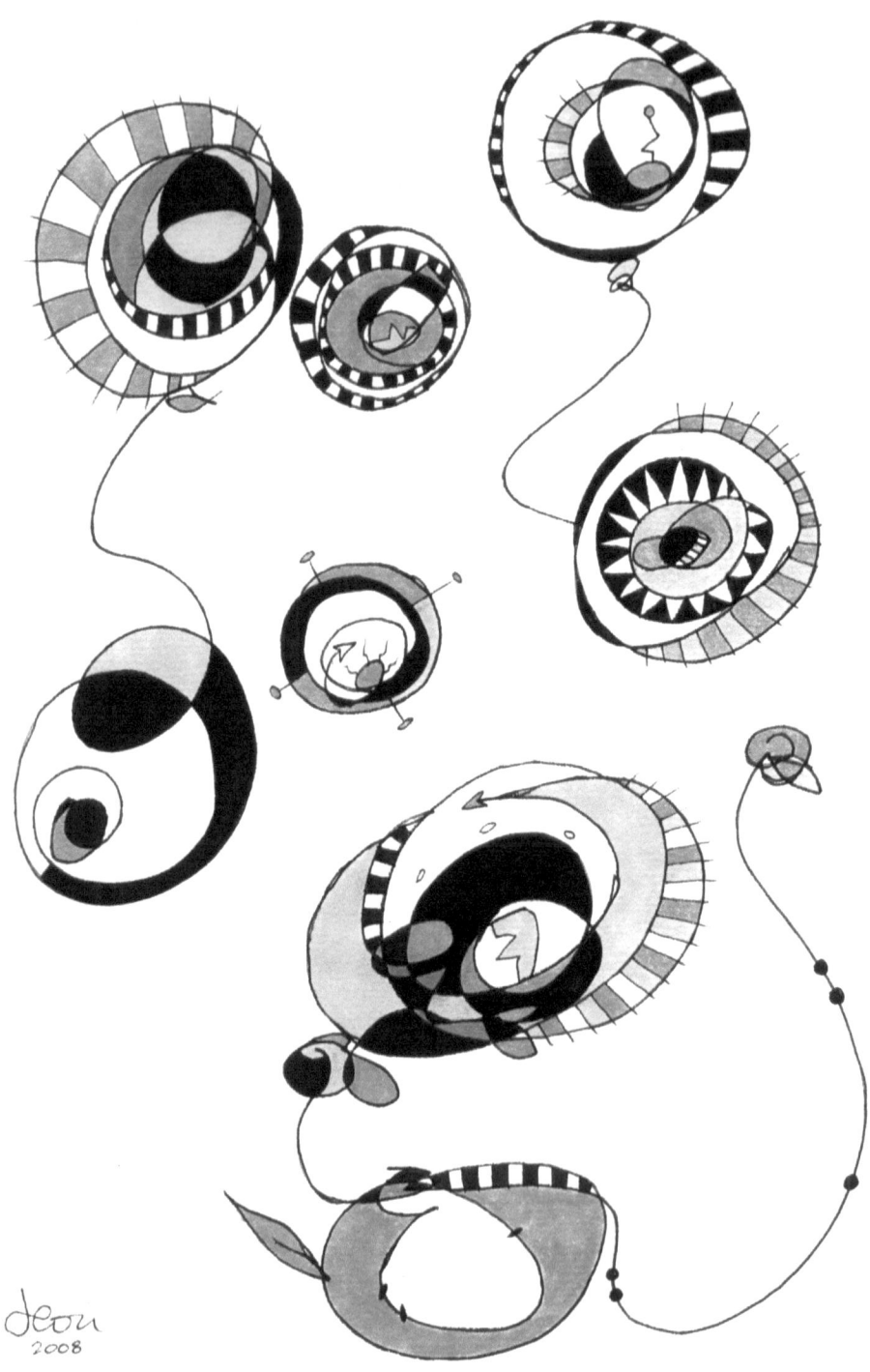

36

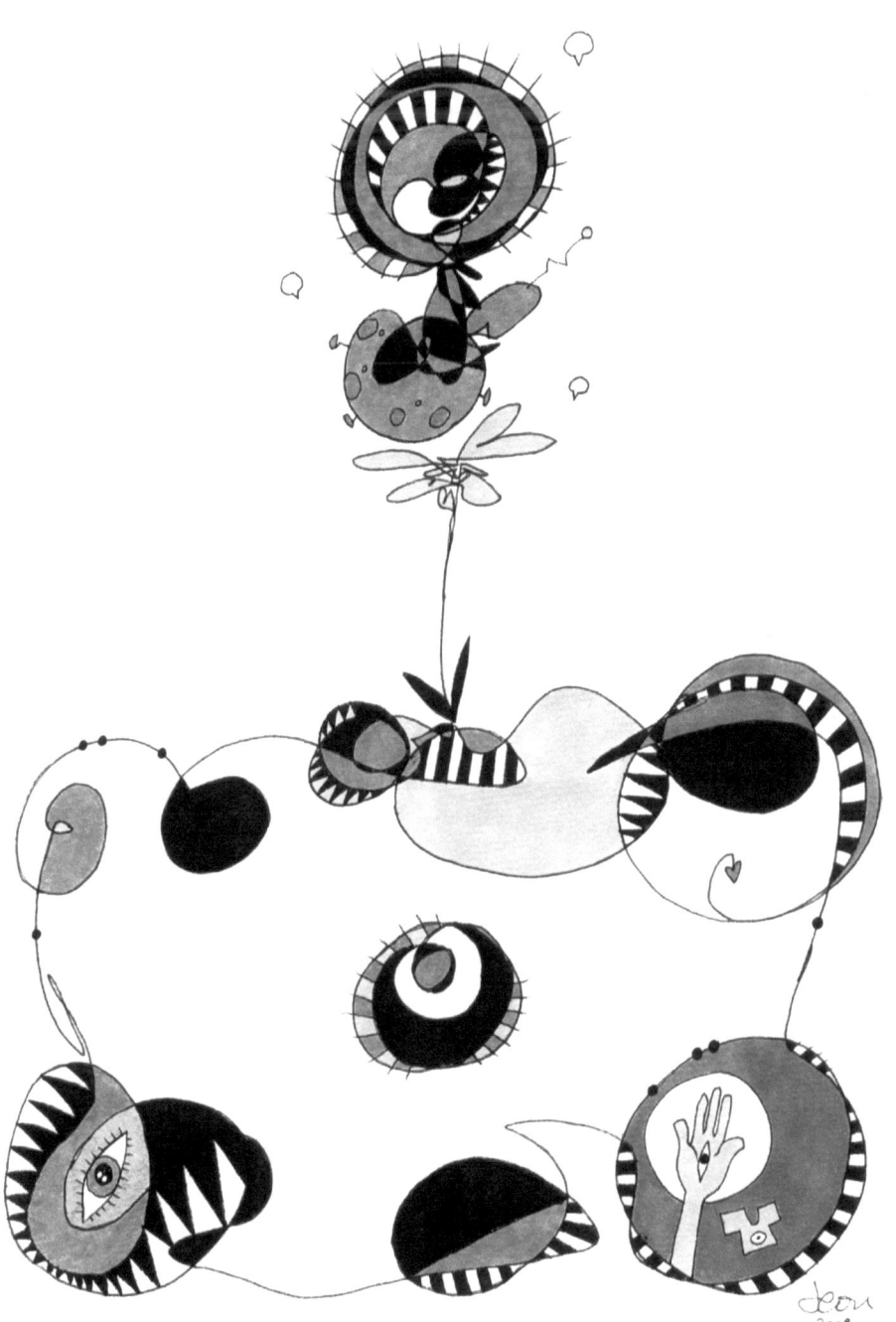

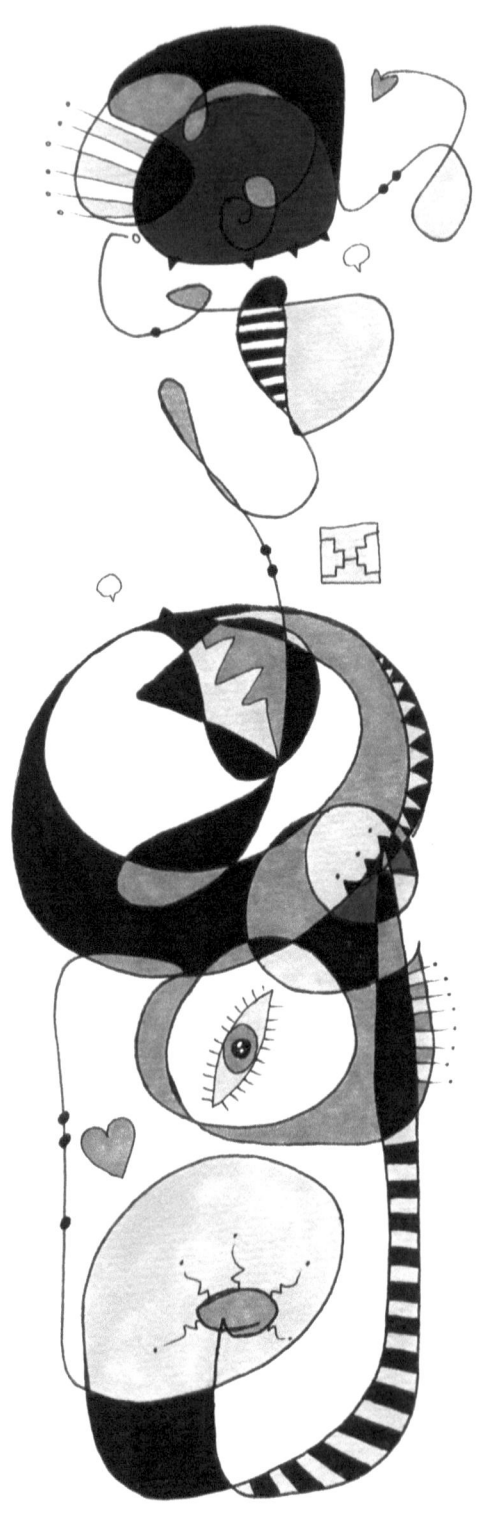

38

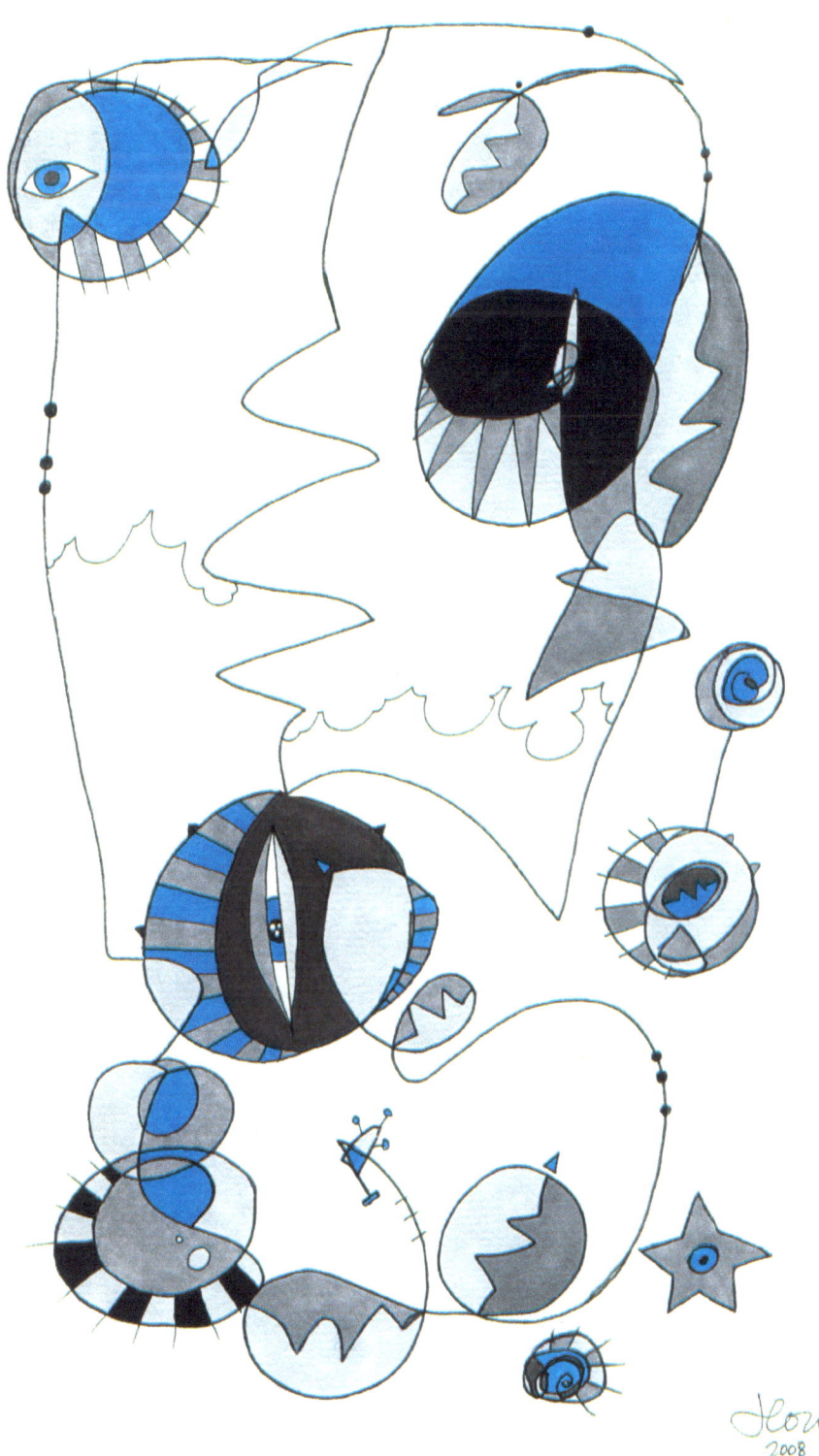

39

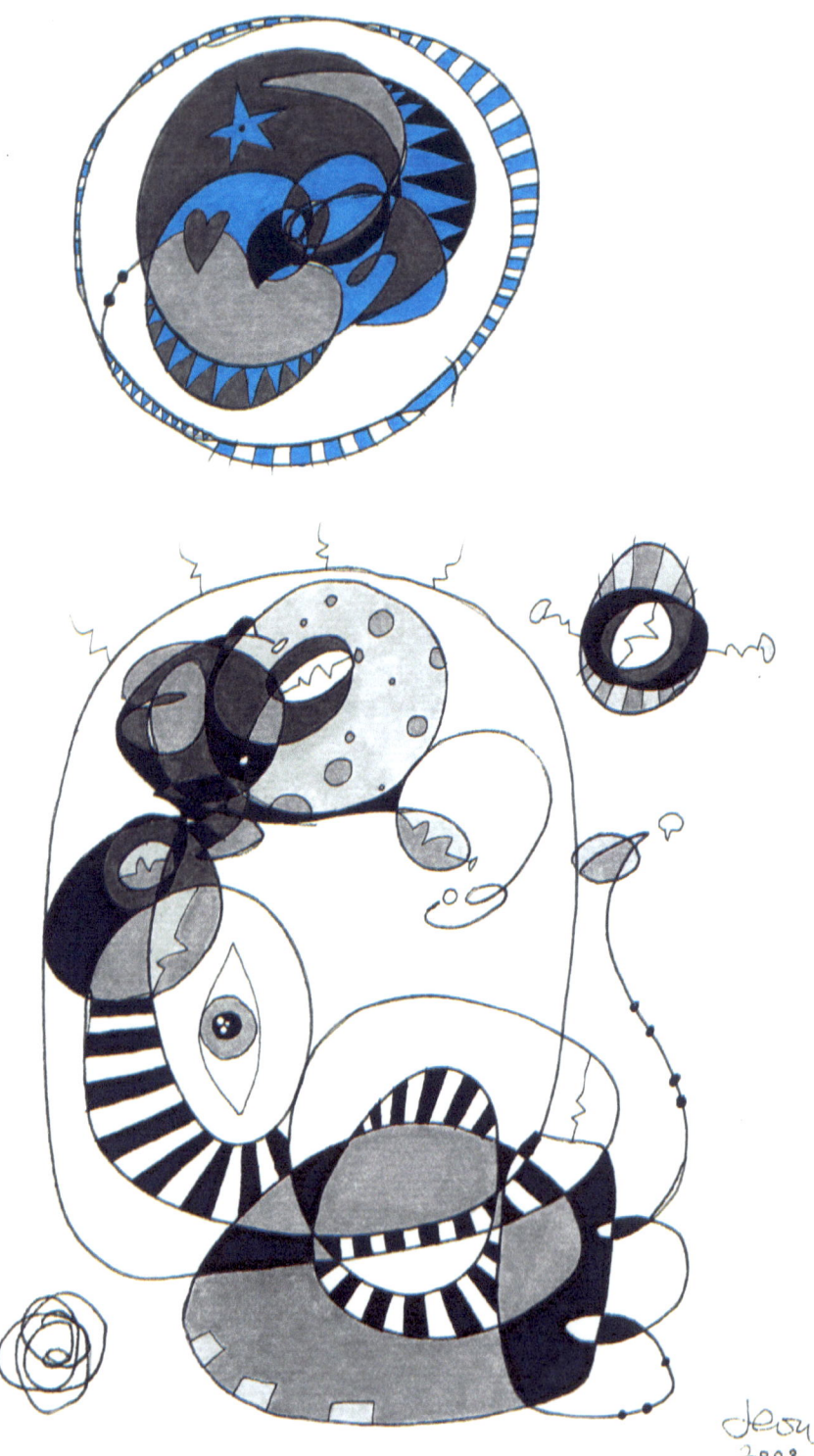

40

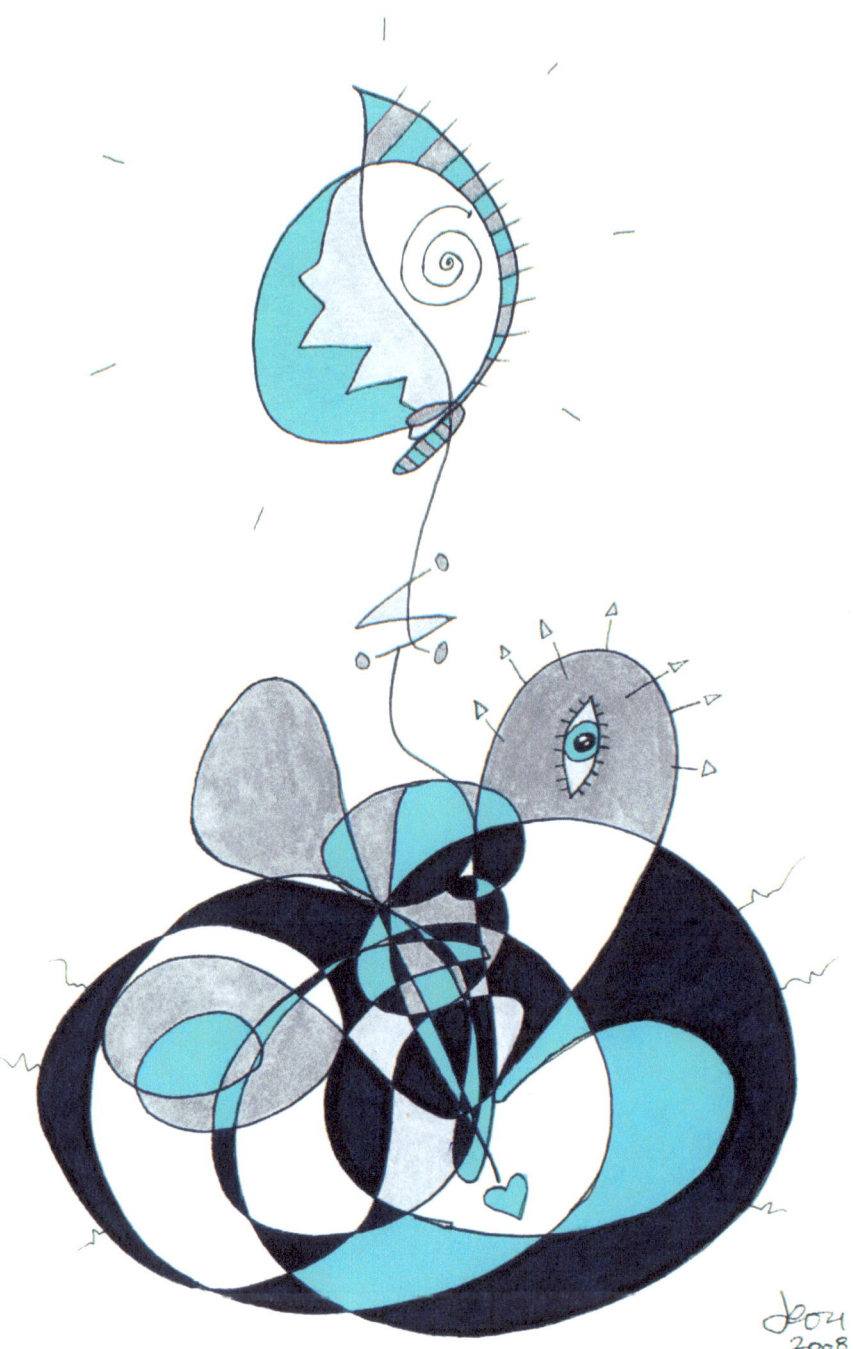

41

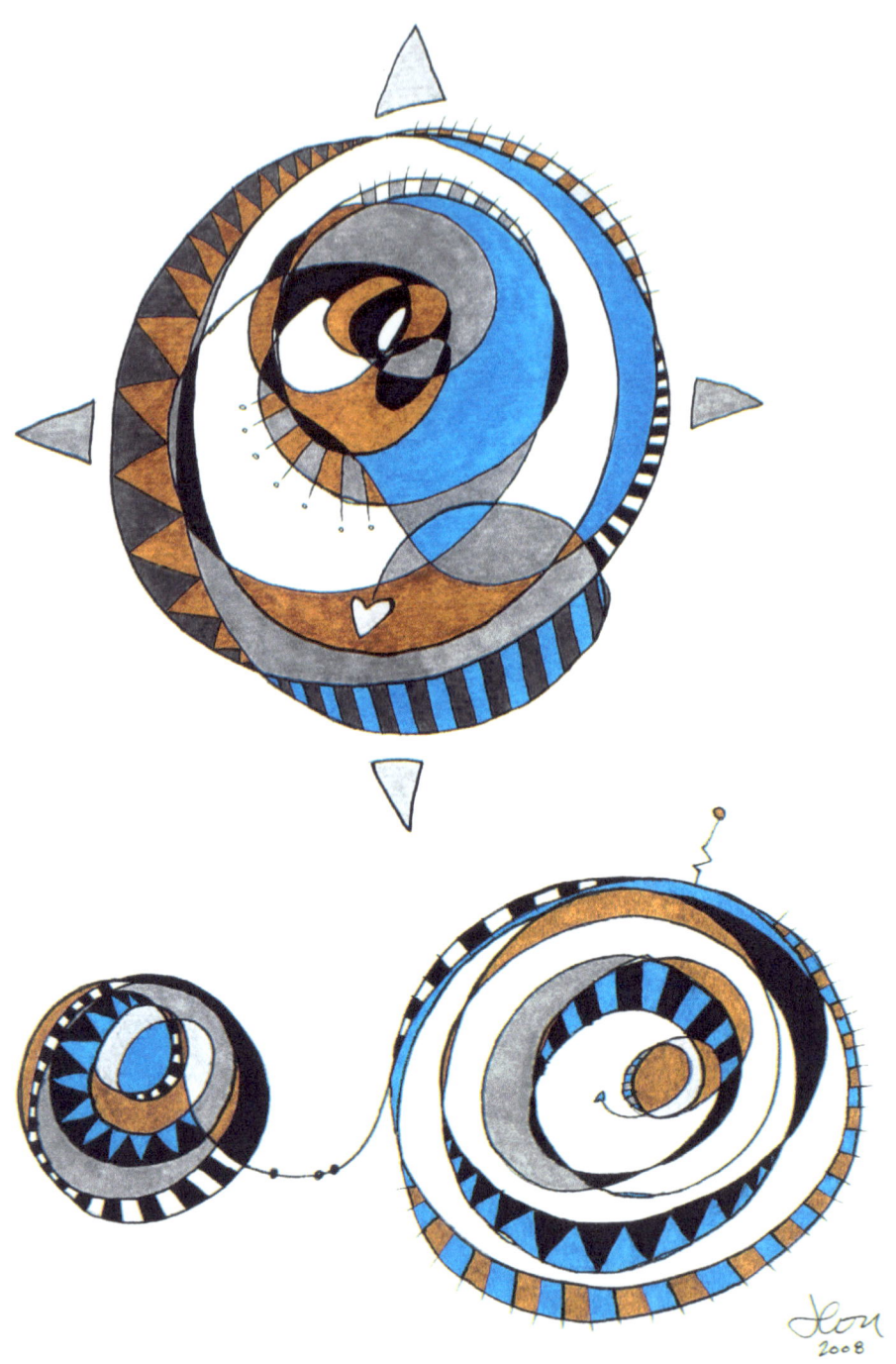

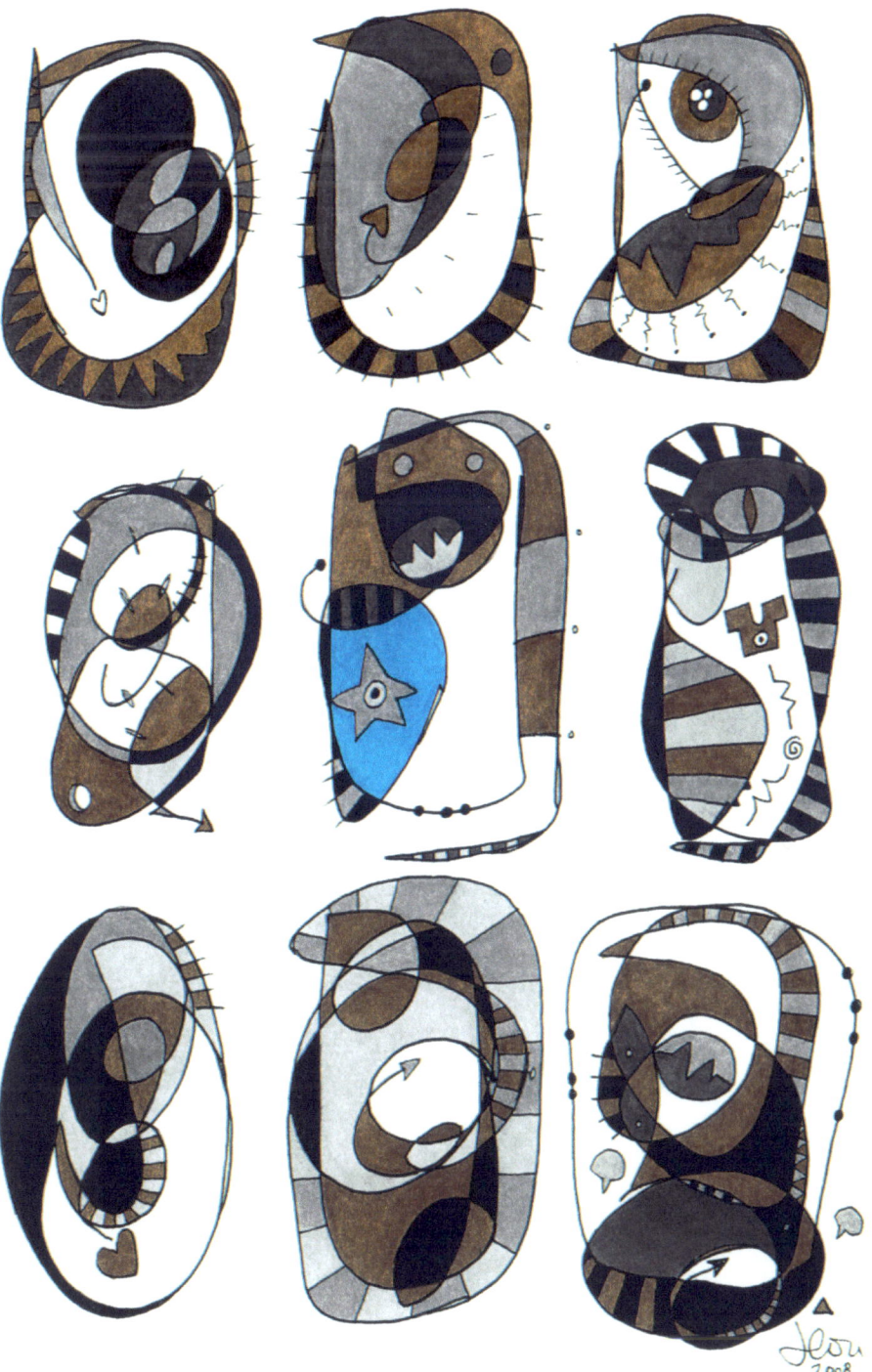

43

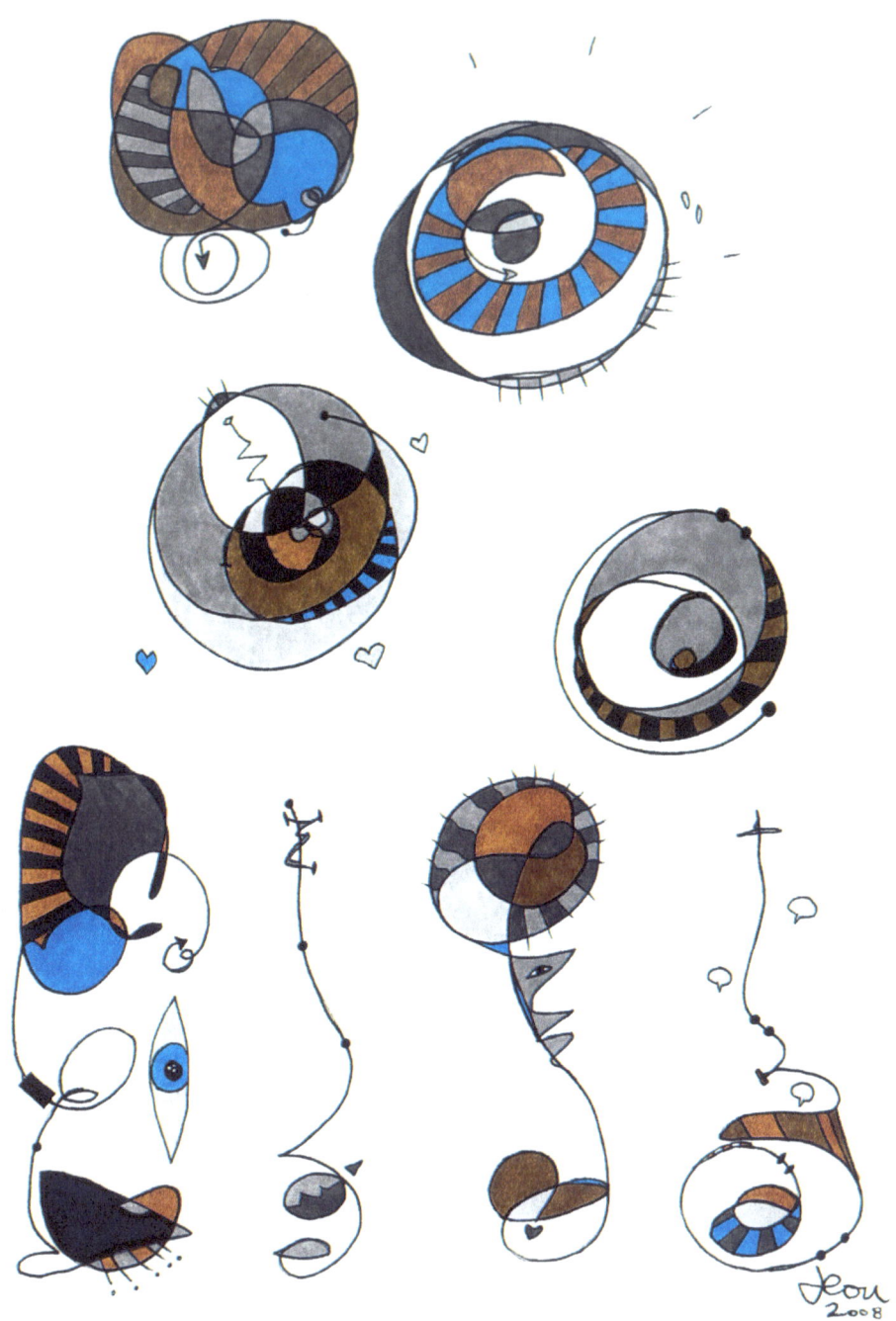

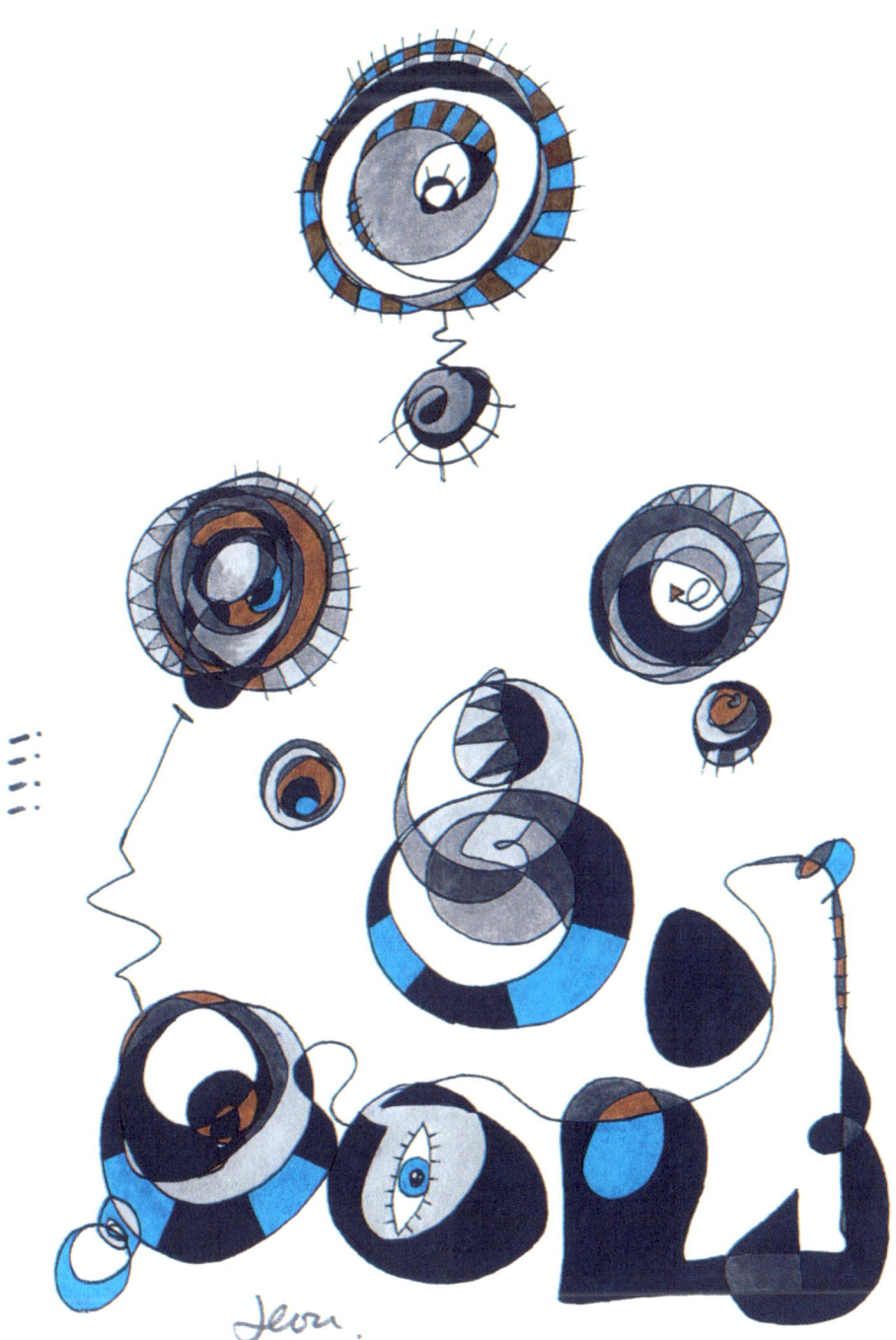

Jean.

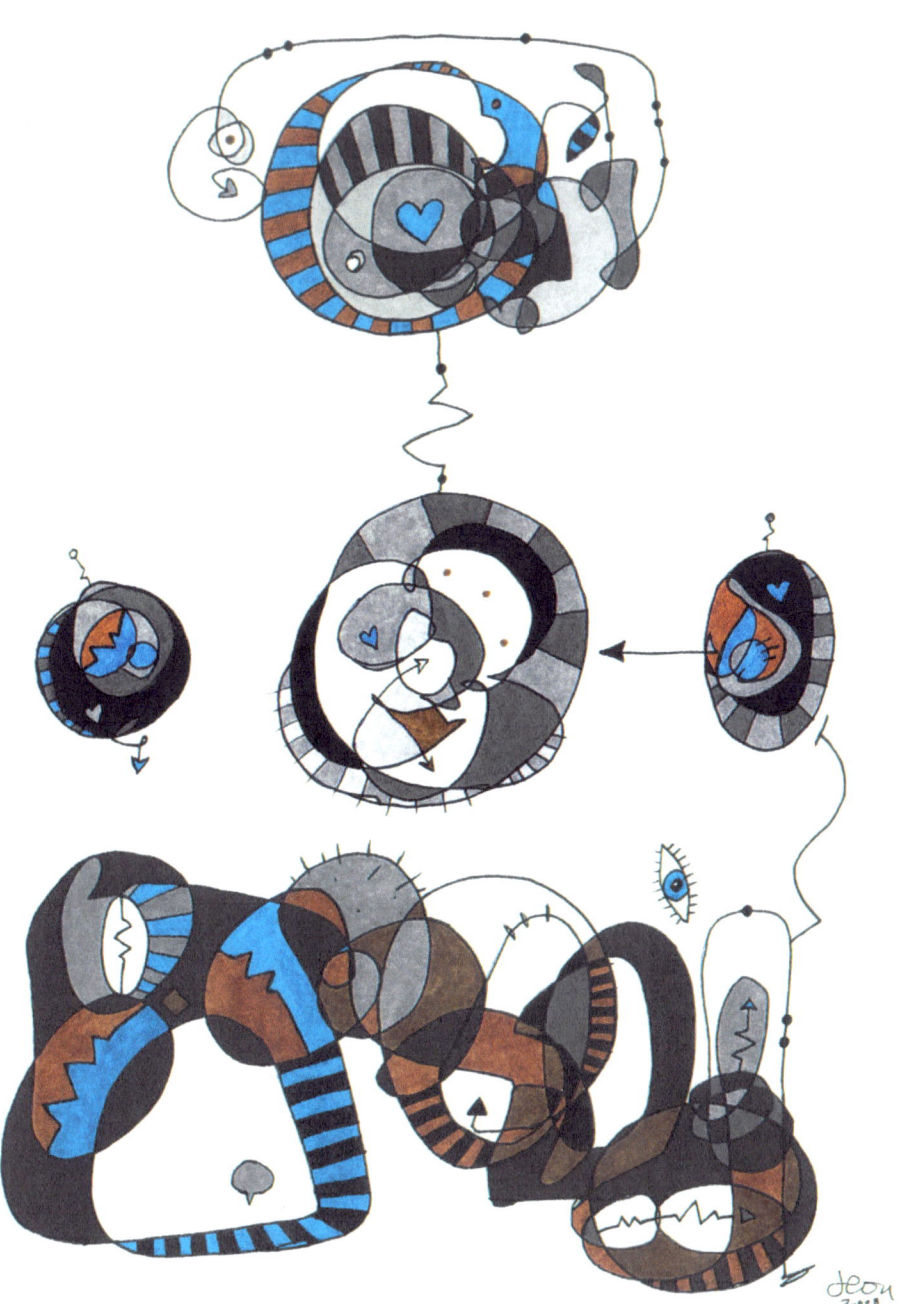

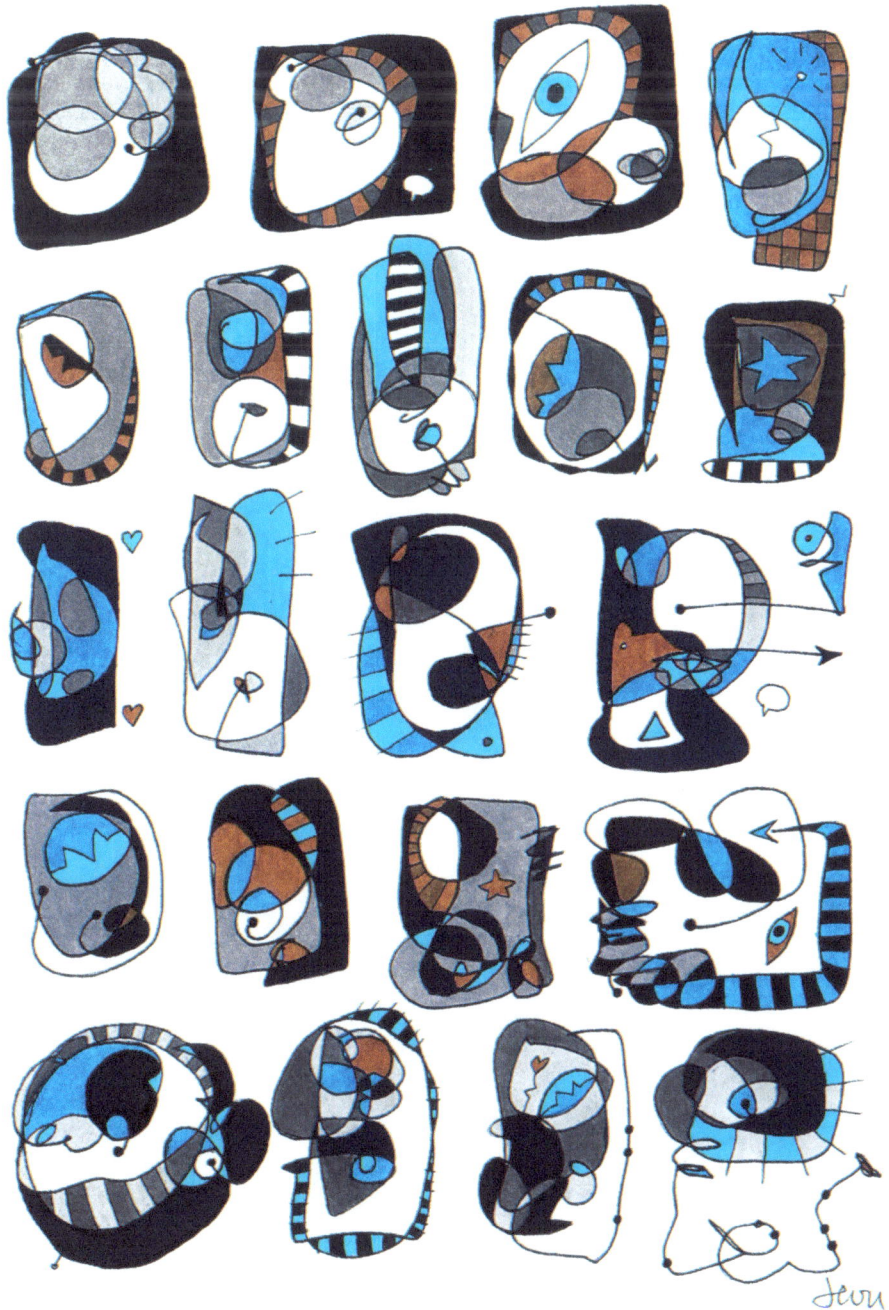

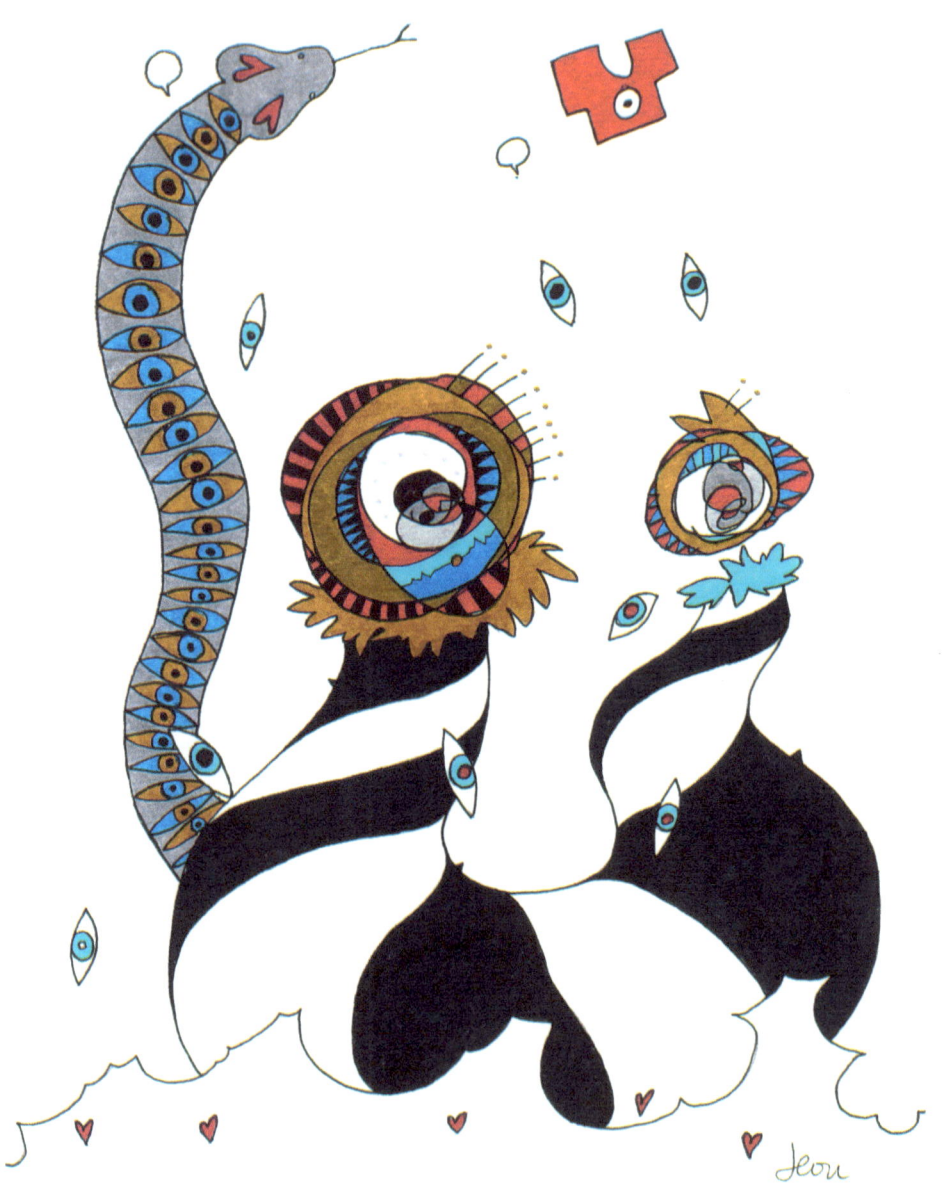

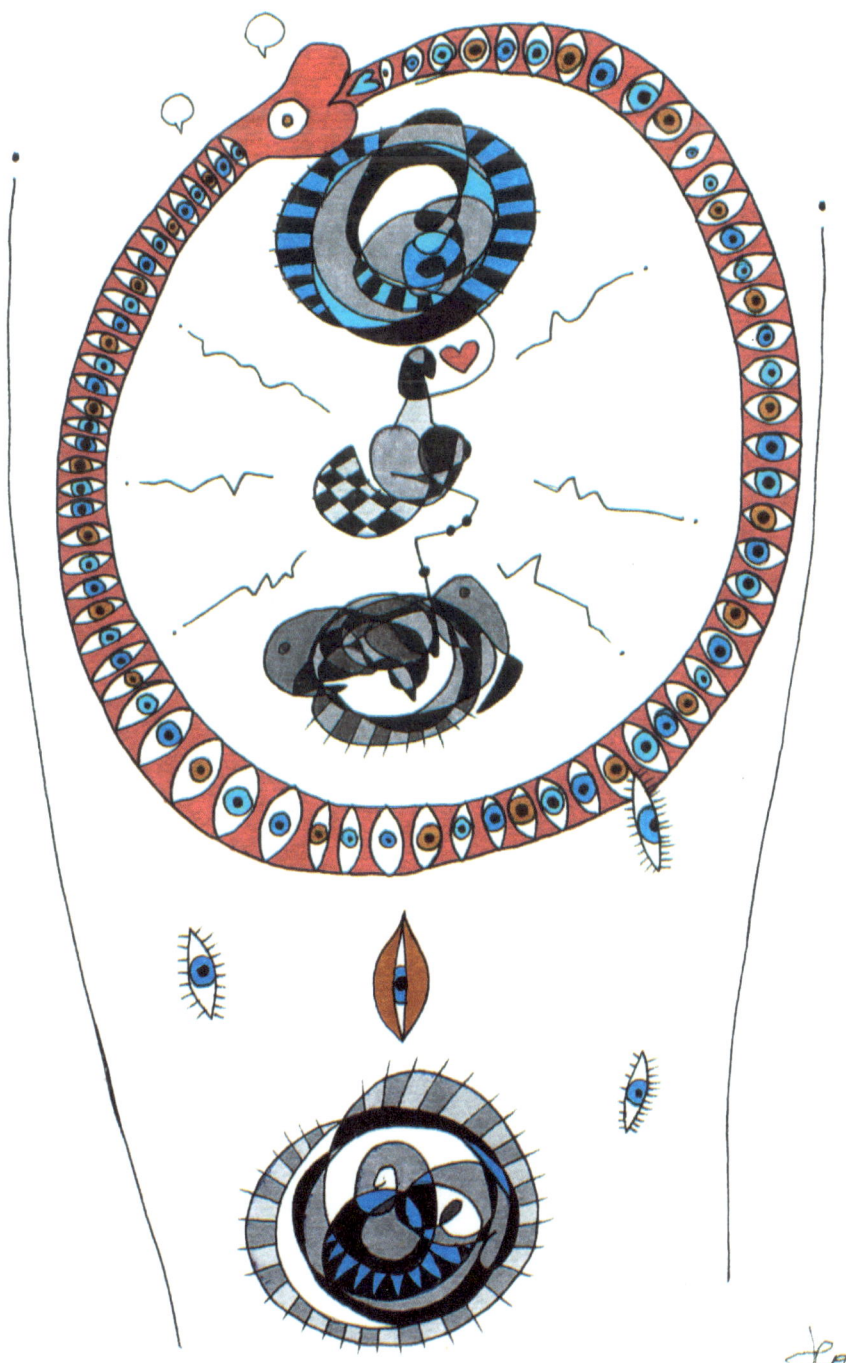

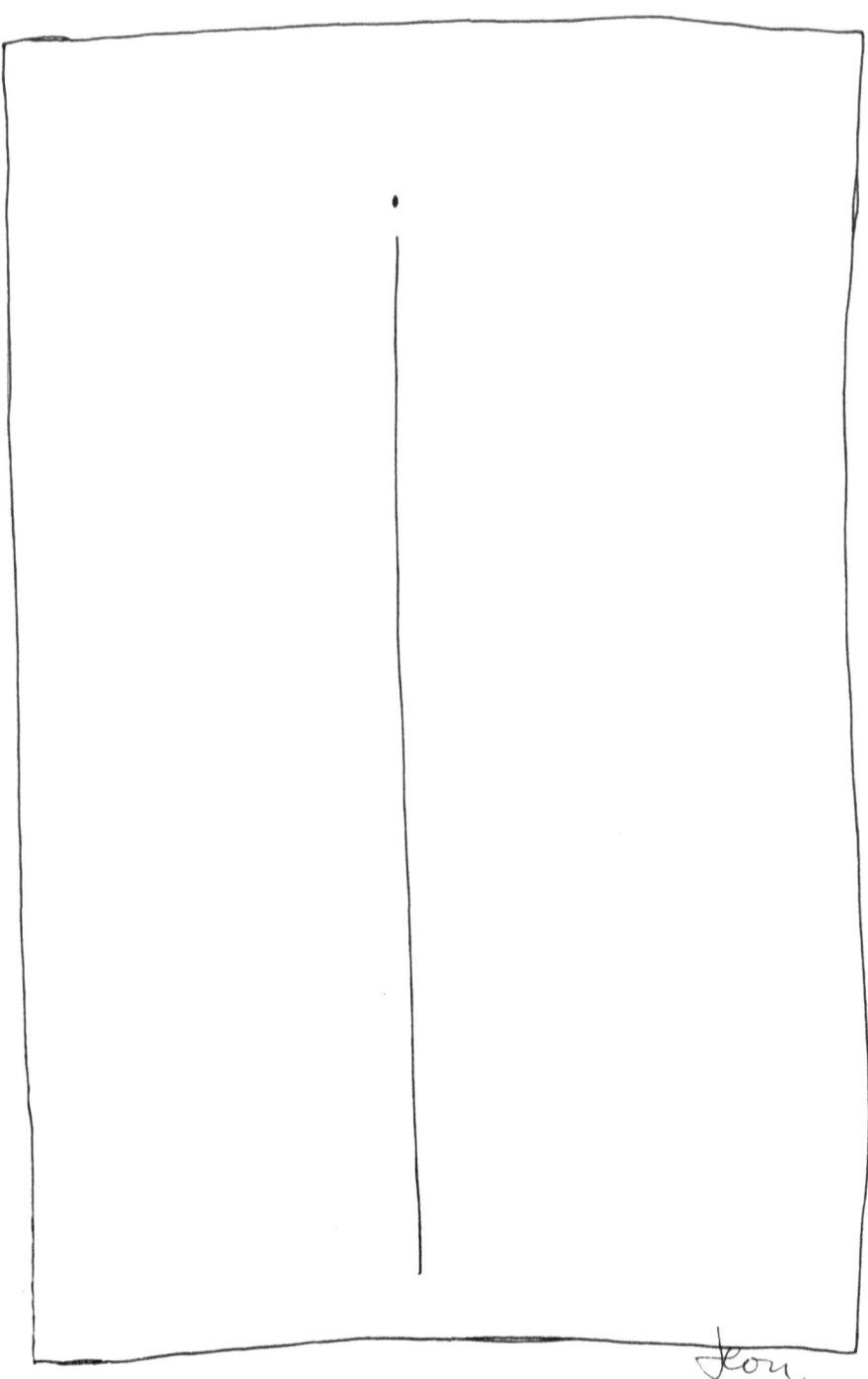

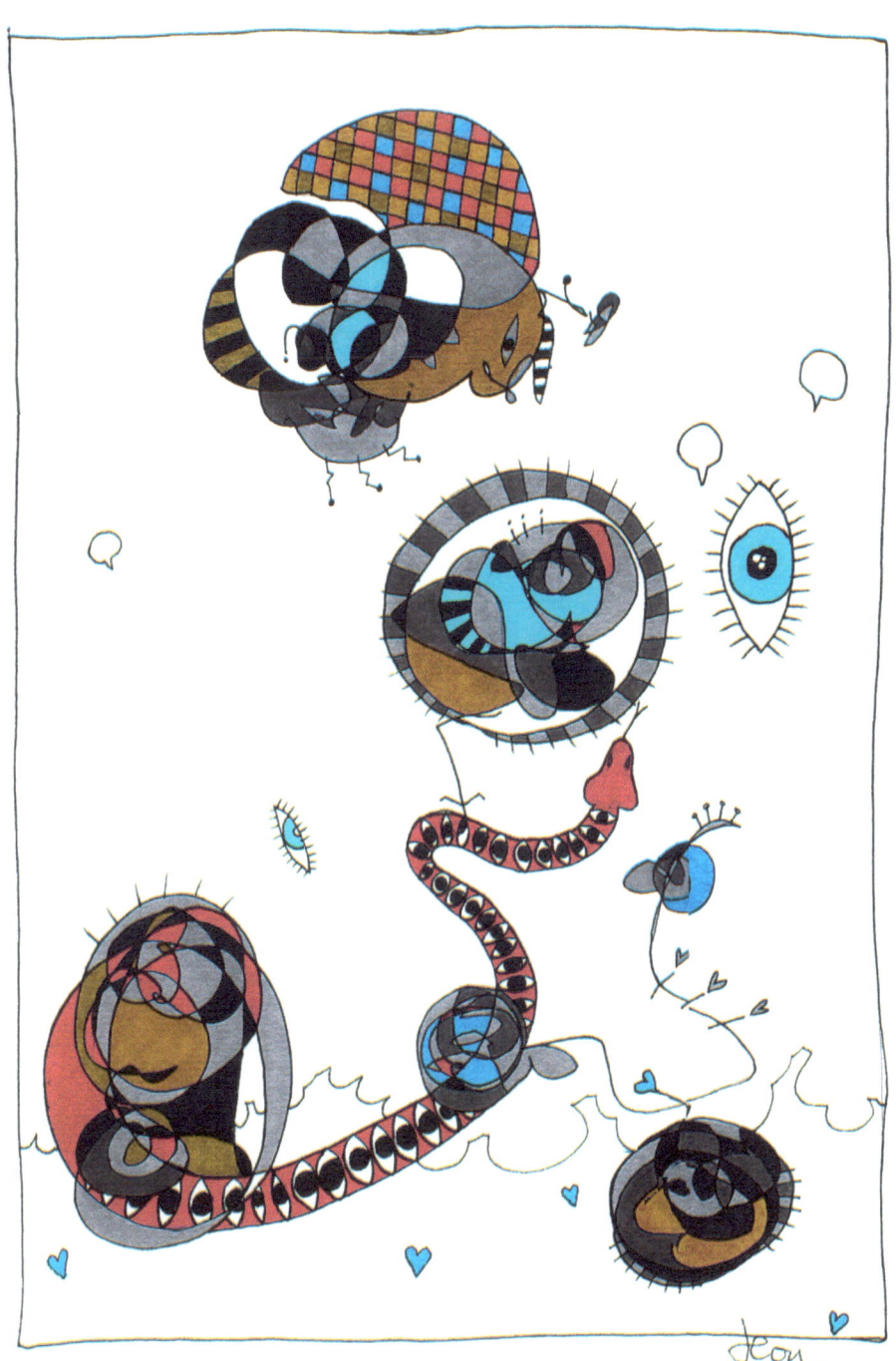

51

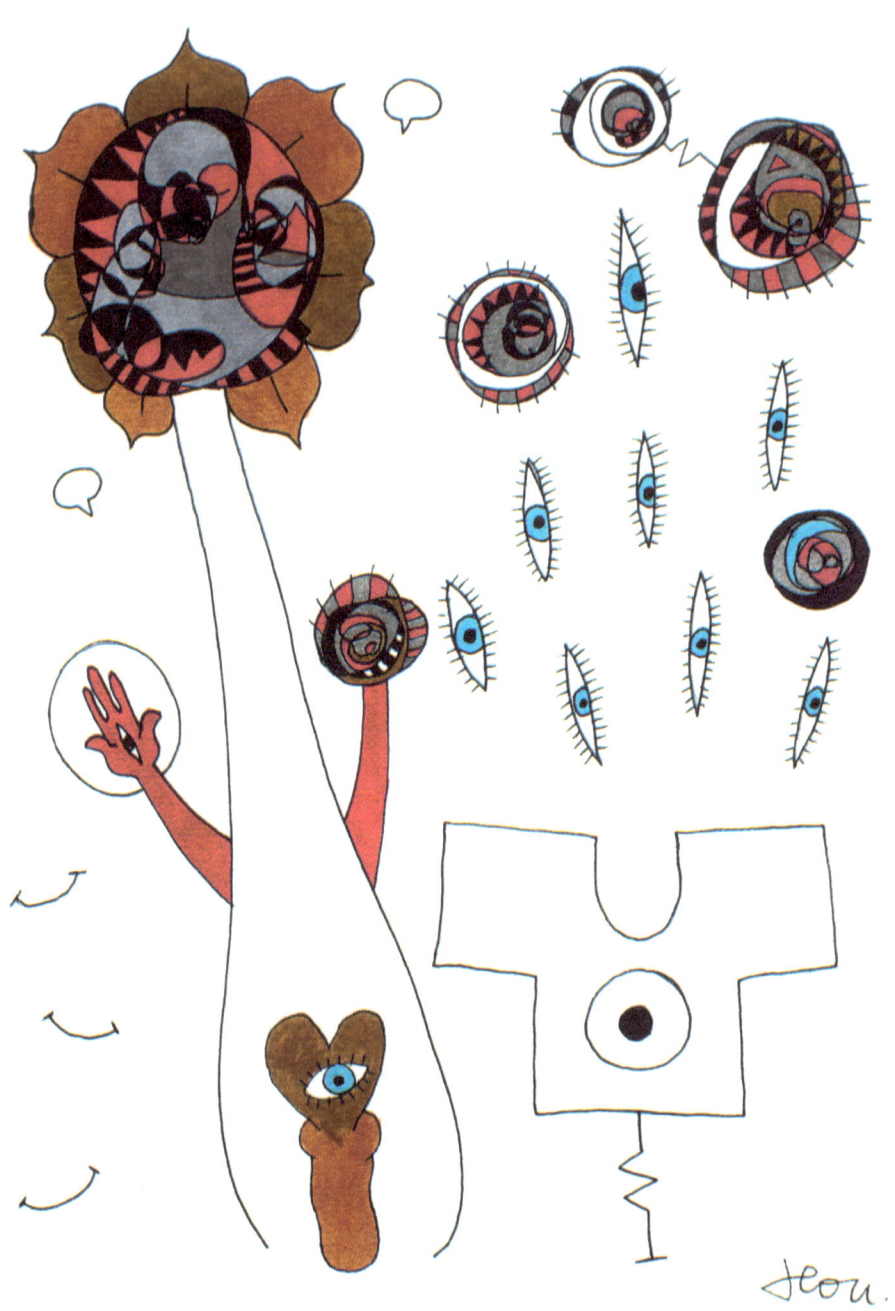

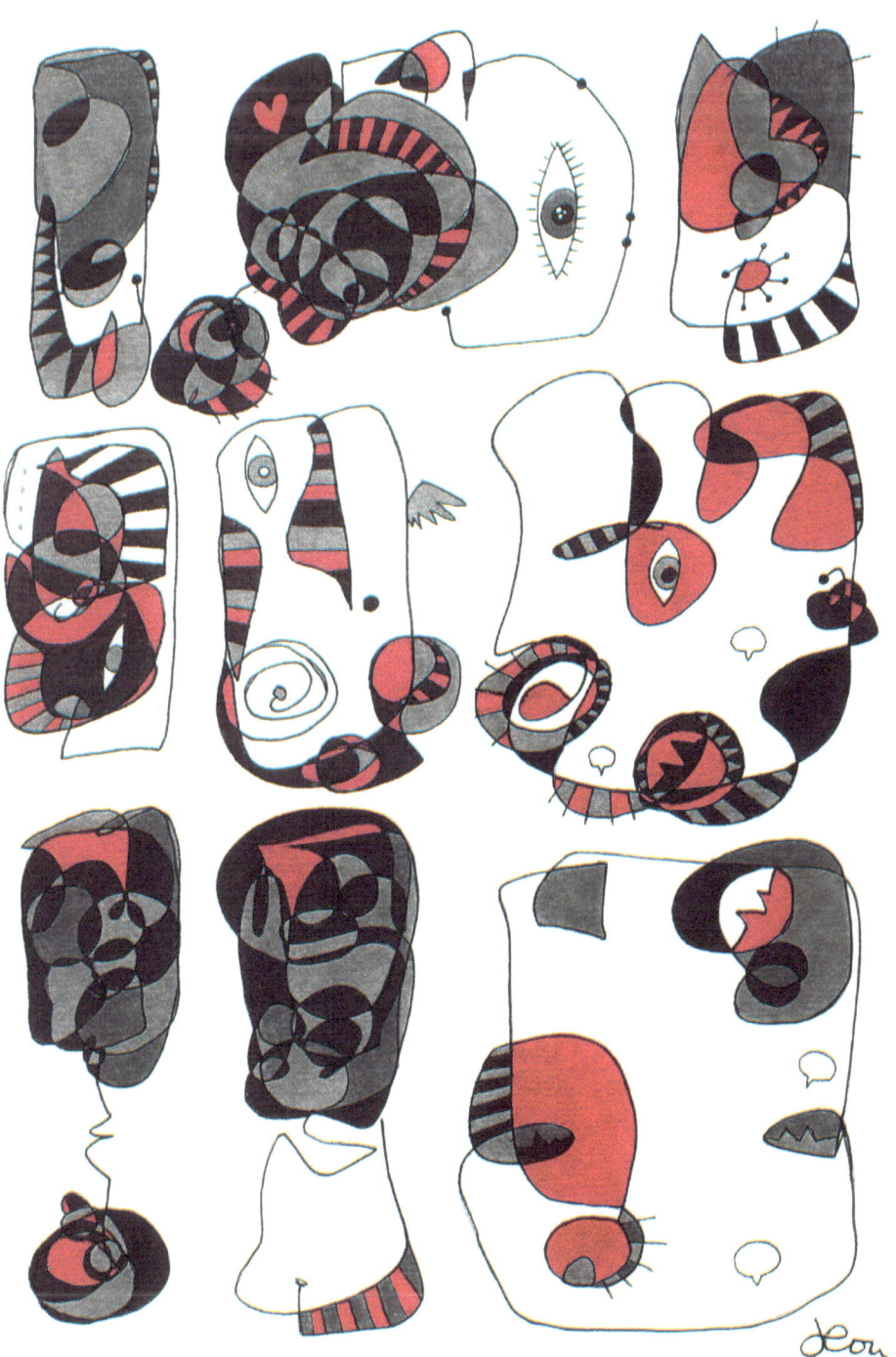

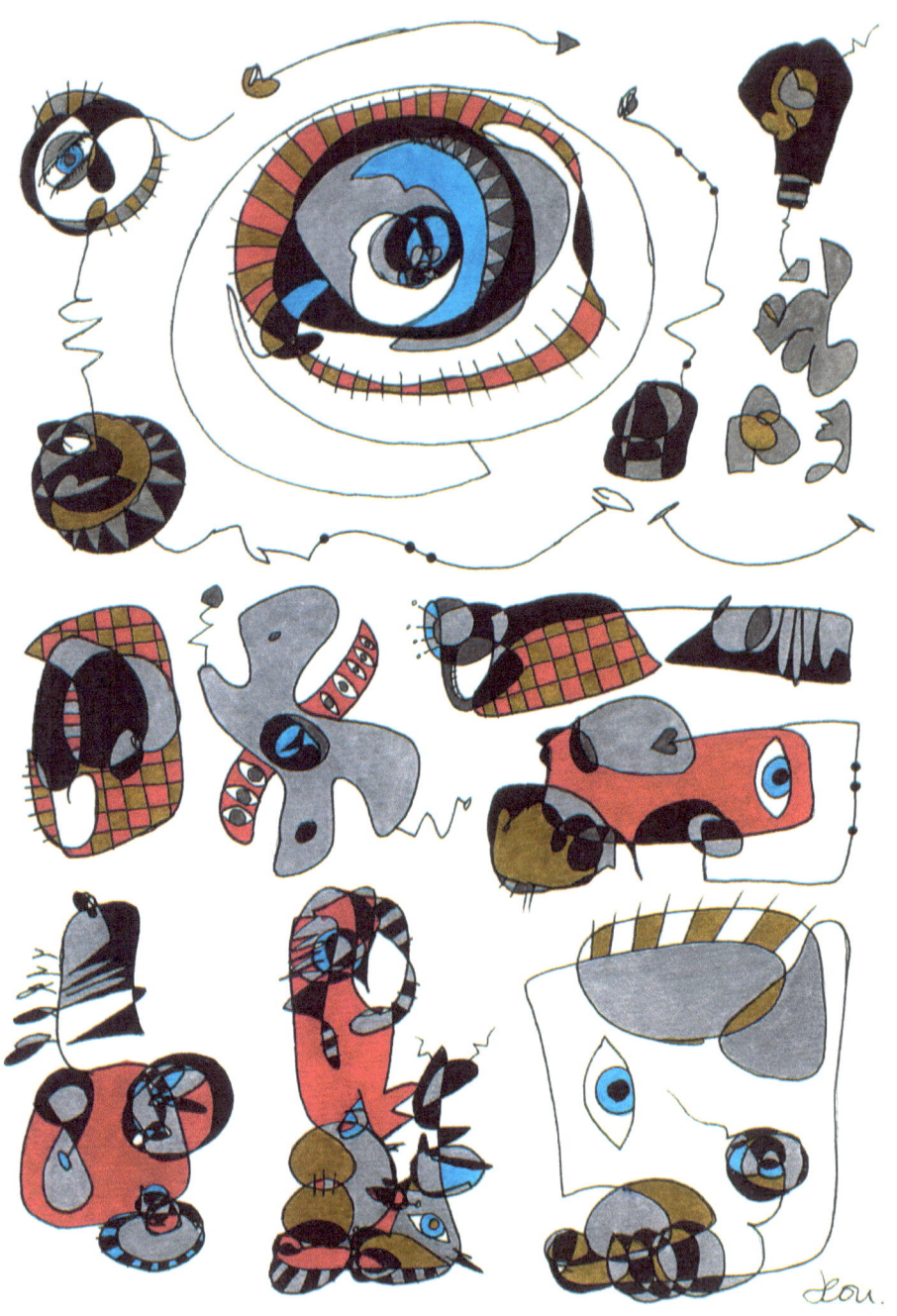

54

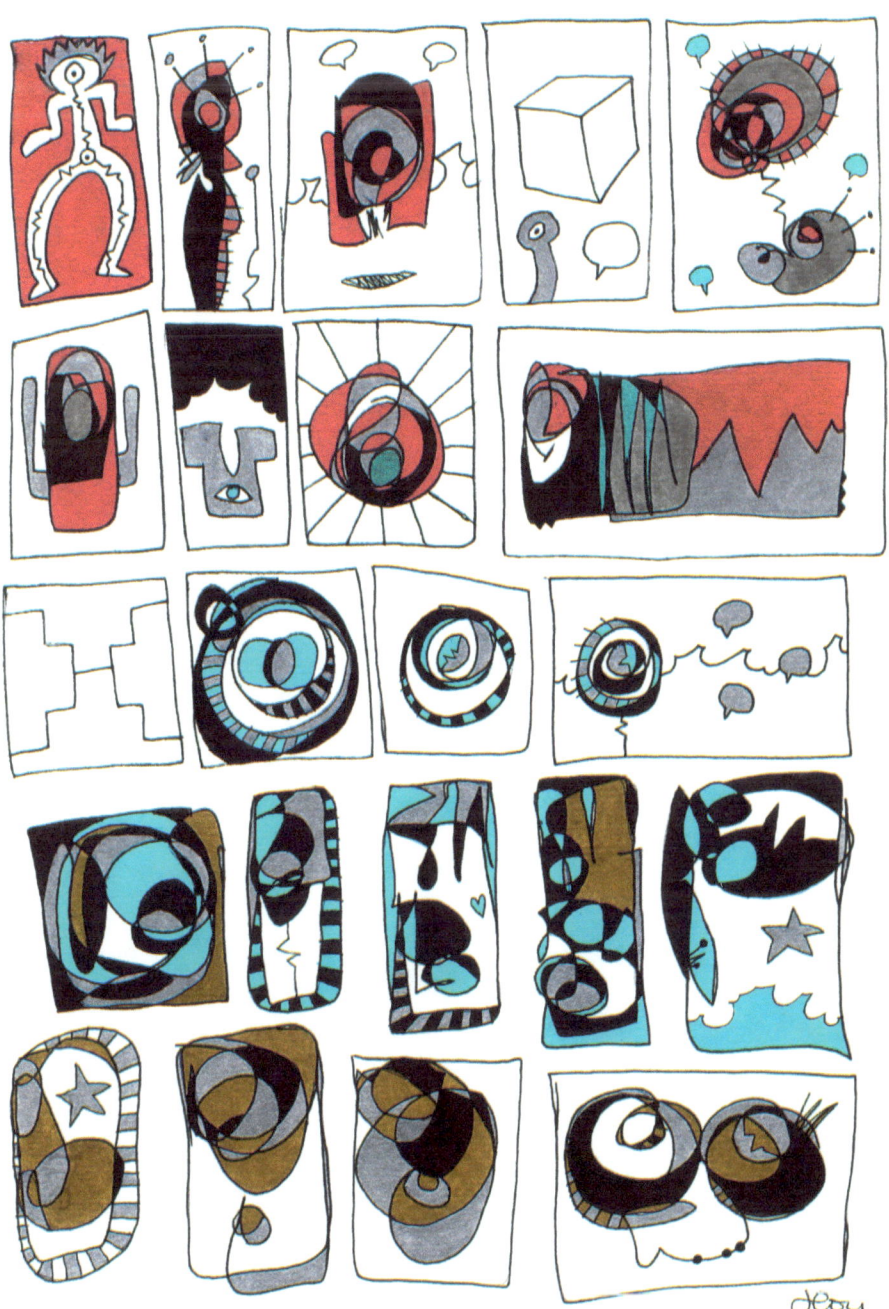

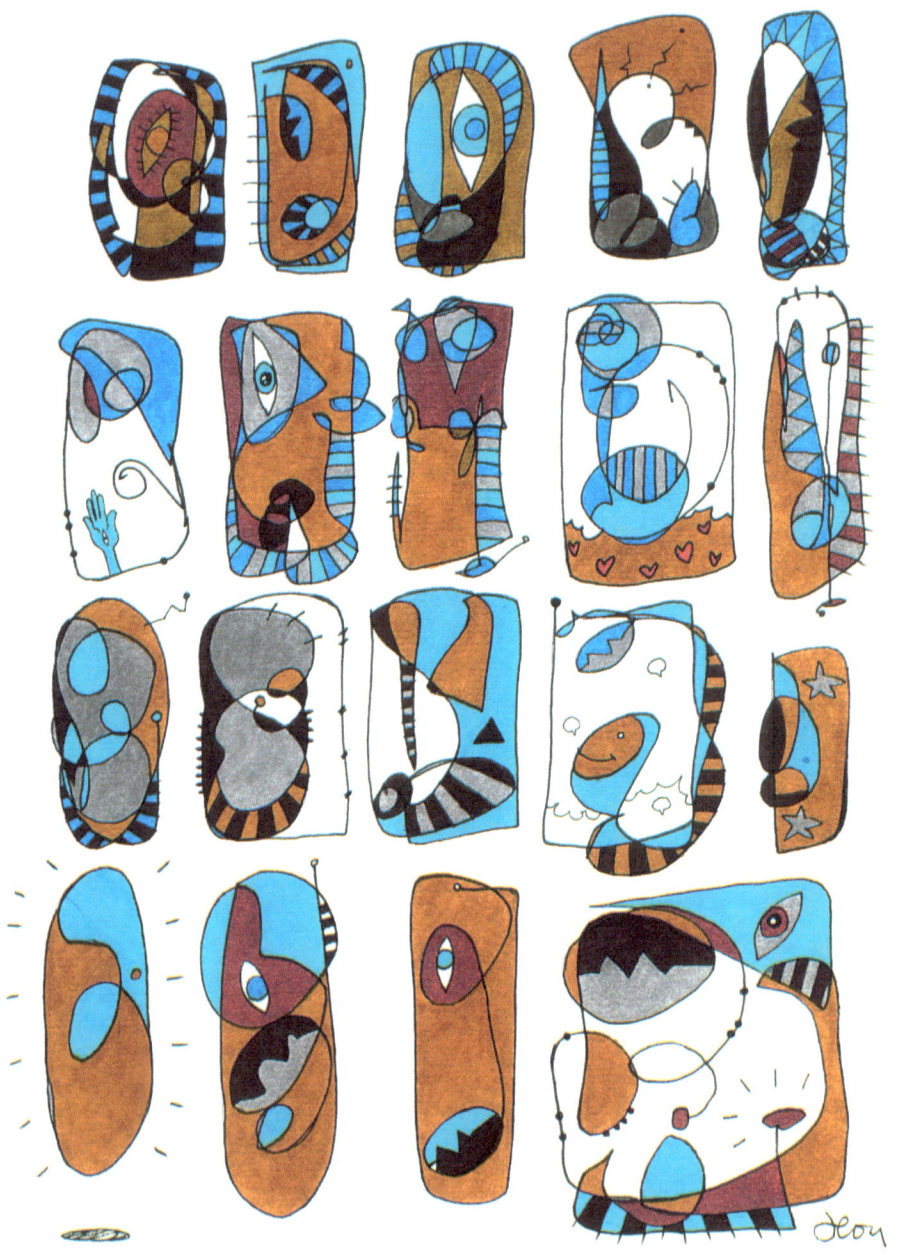

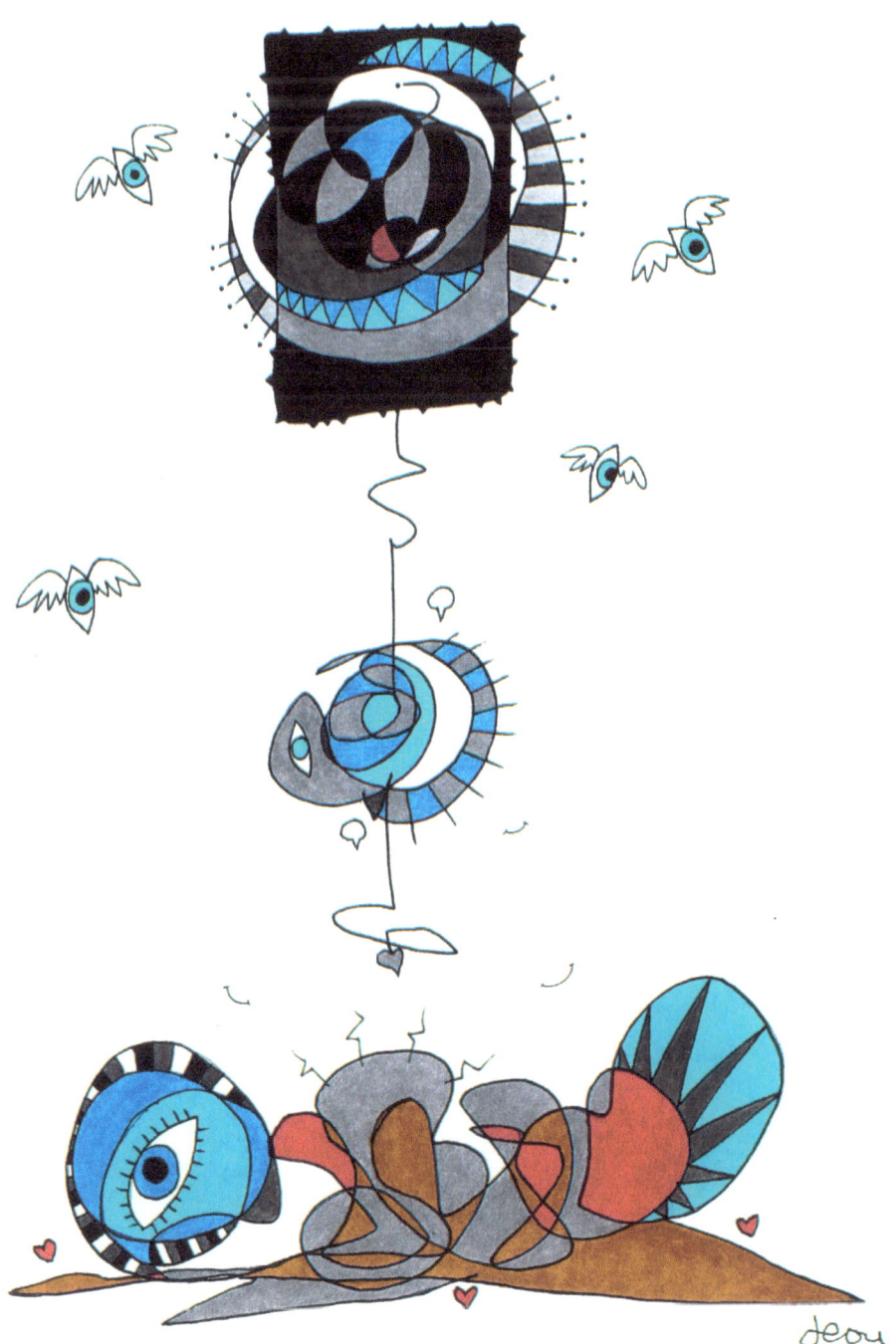

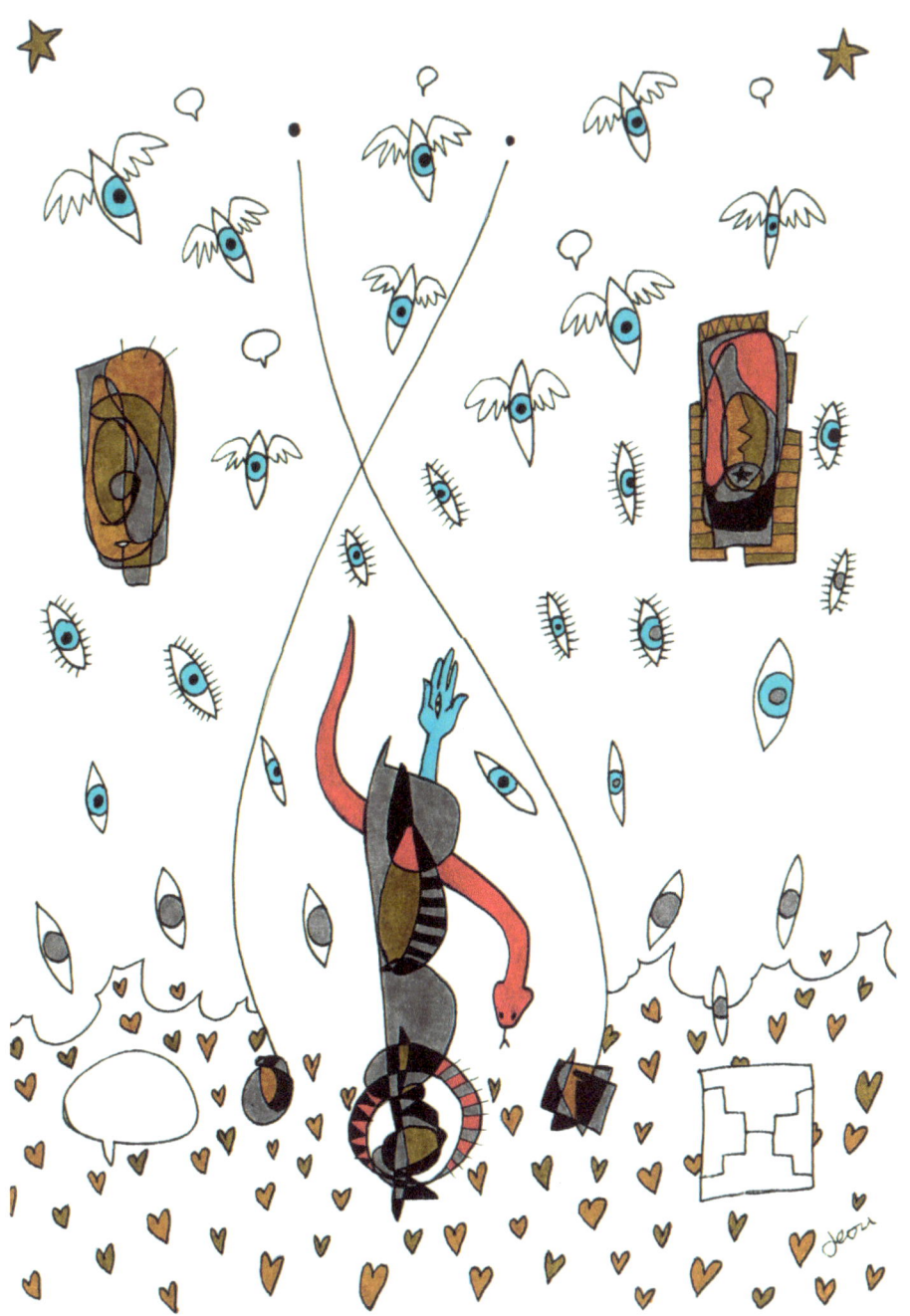

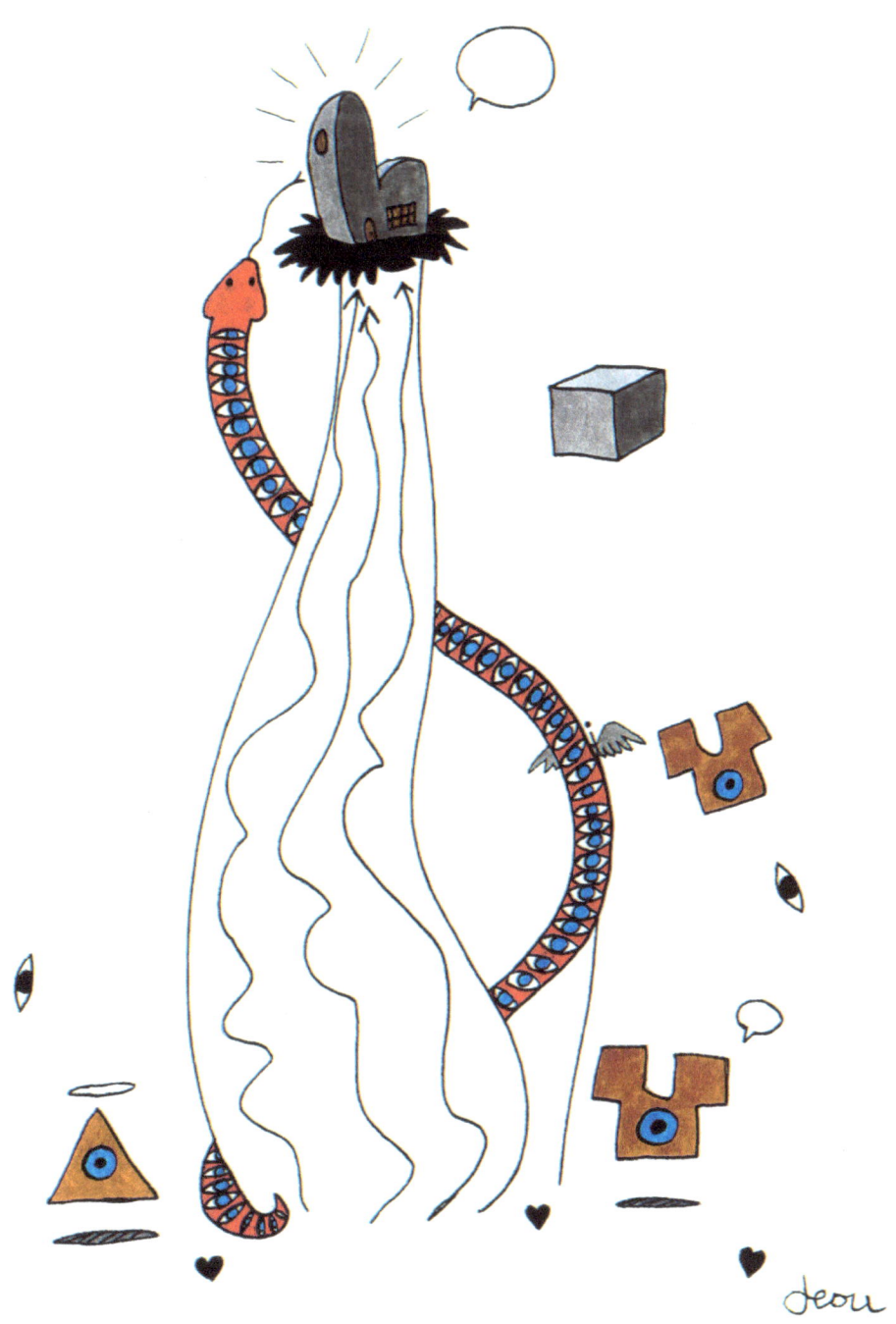

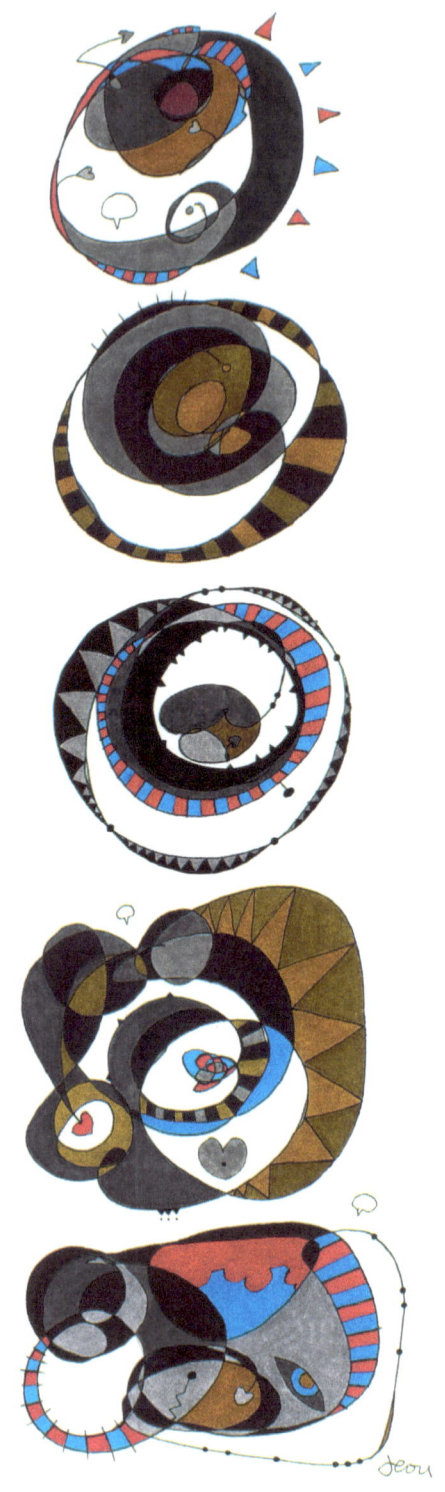

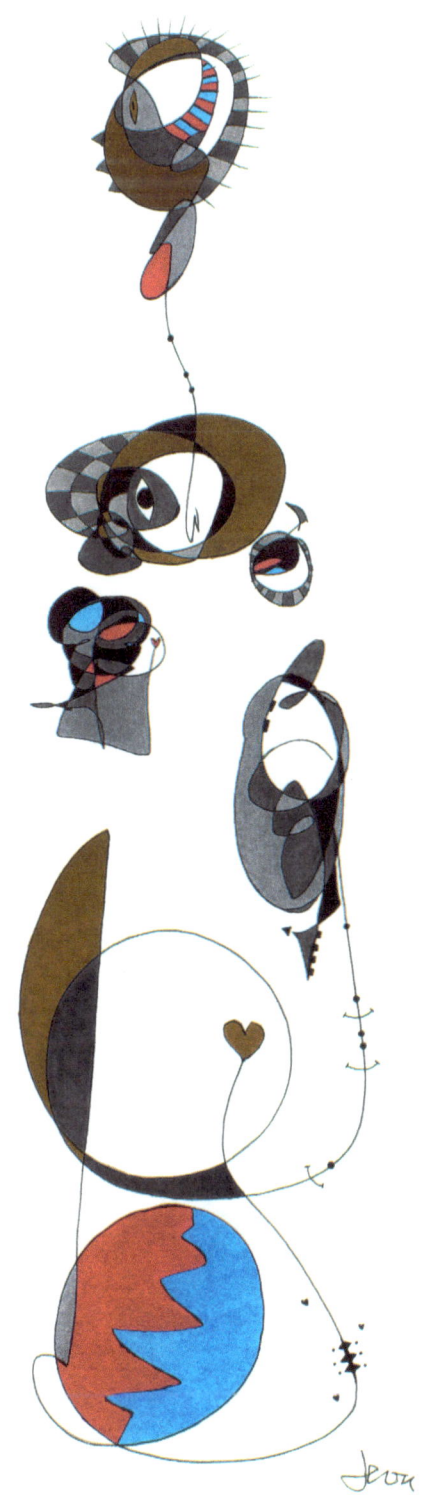

61

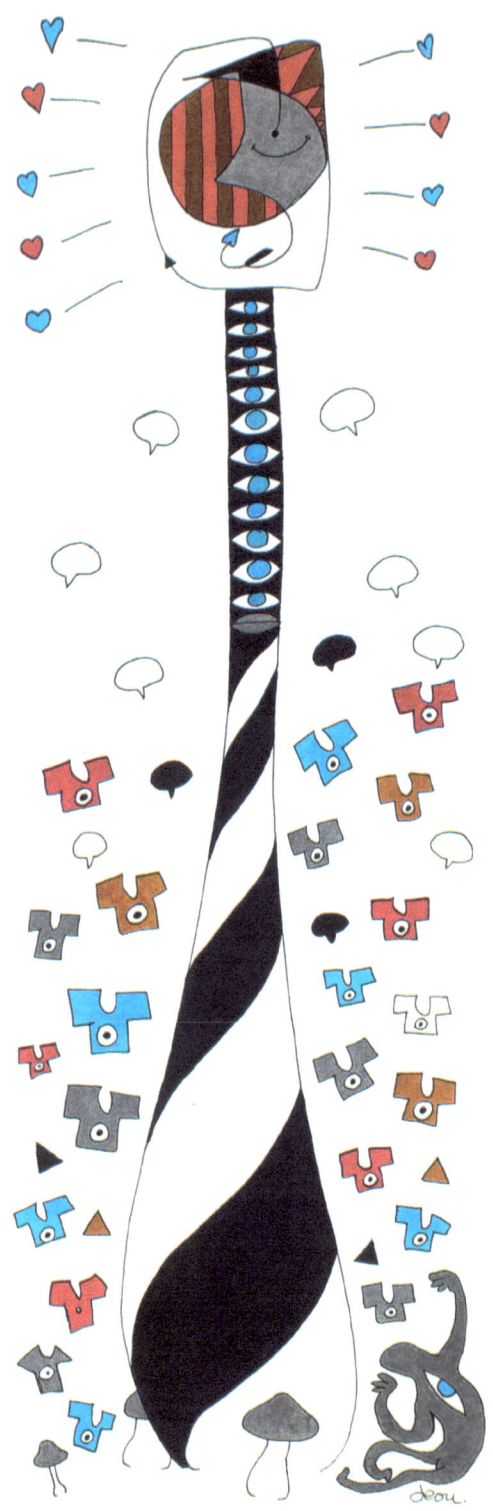

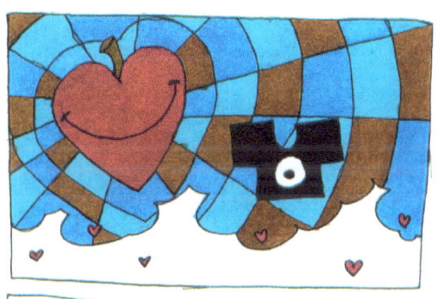

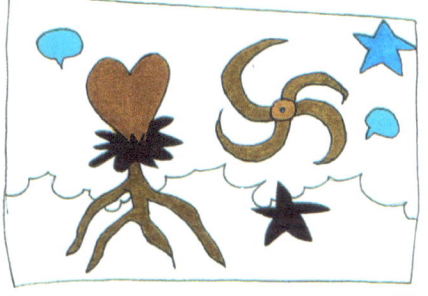

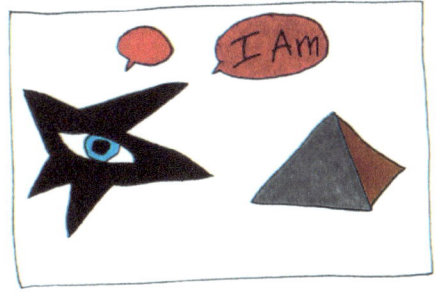

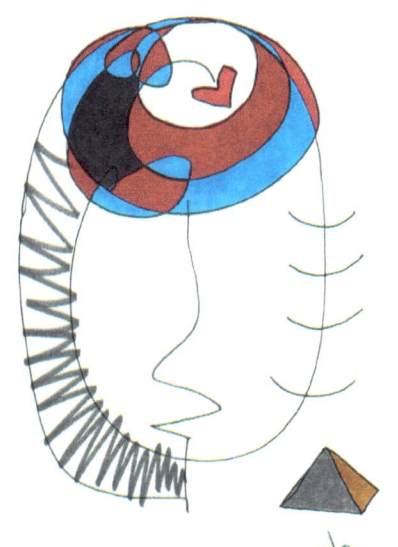

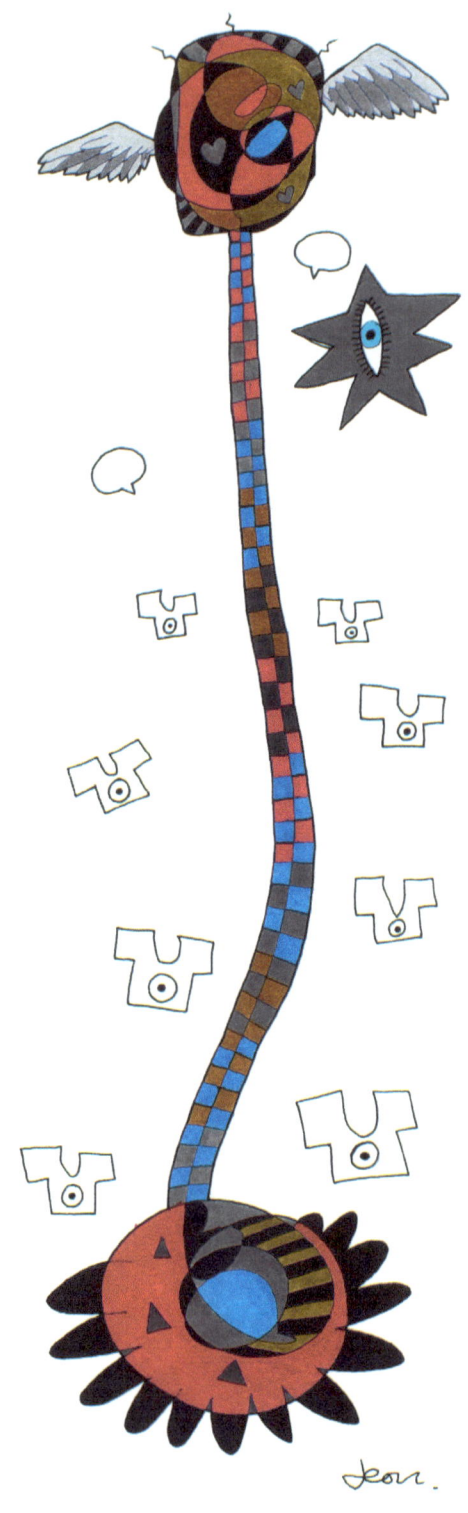

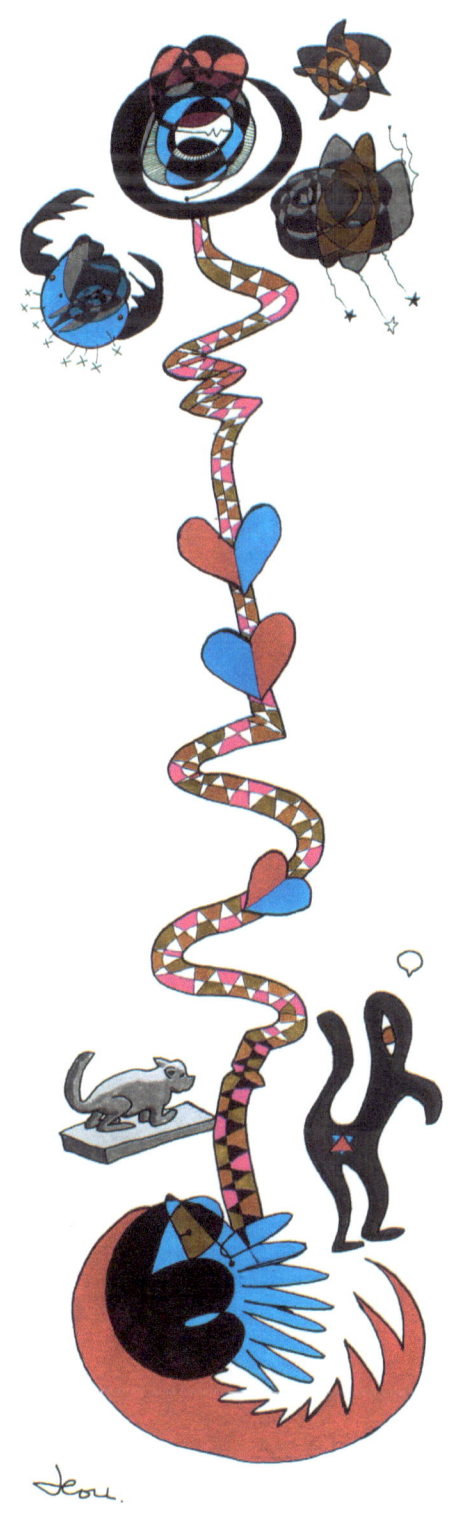

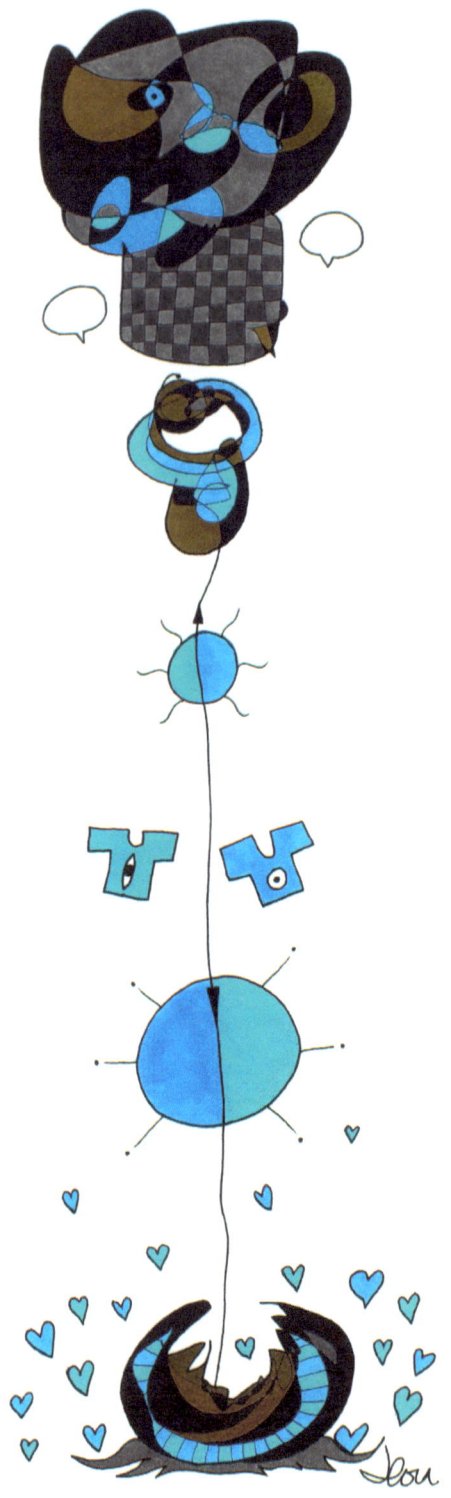

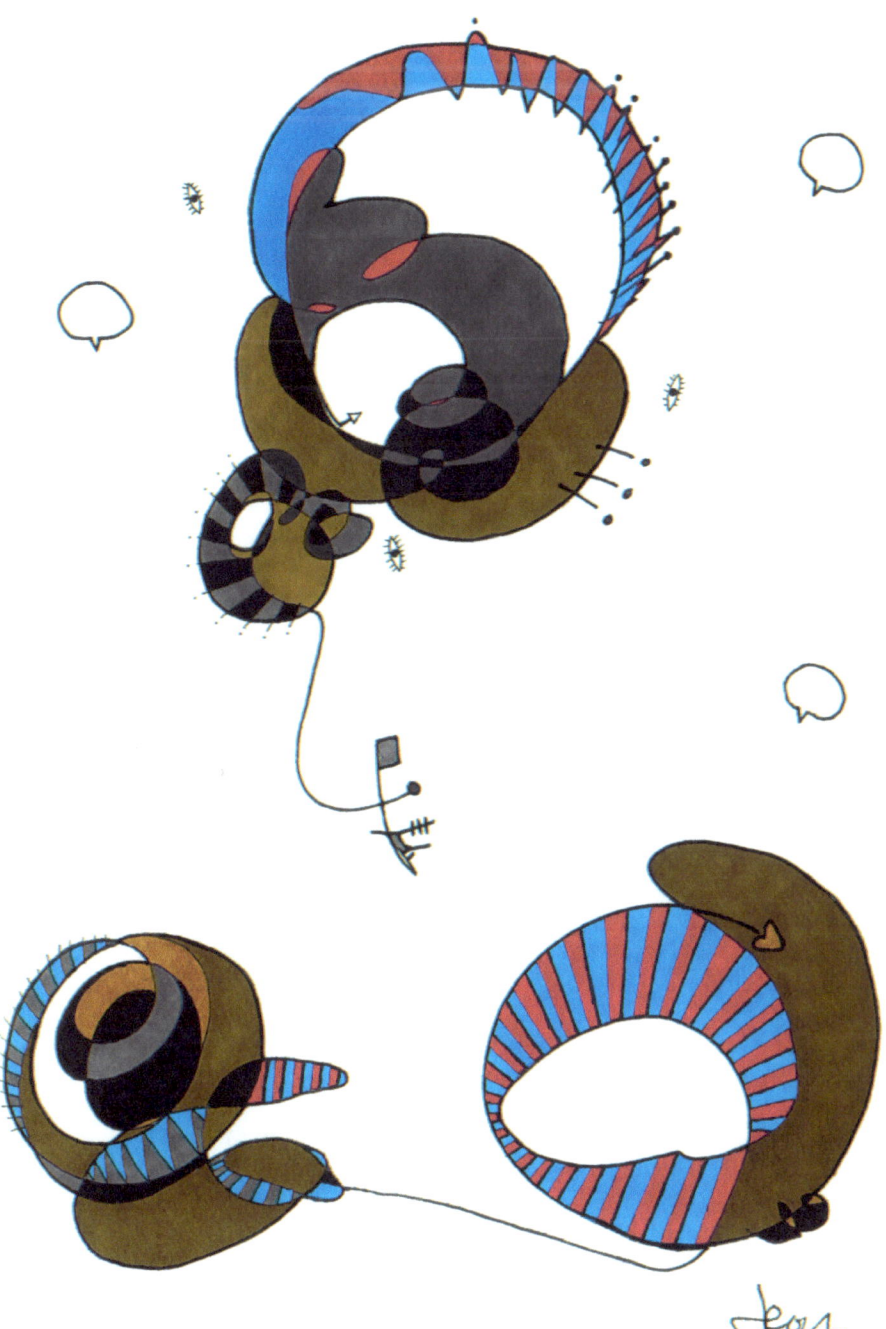

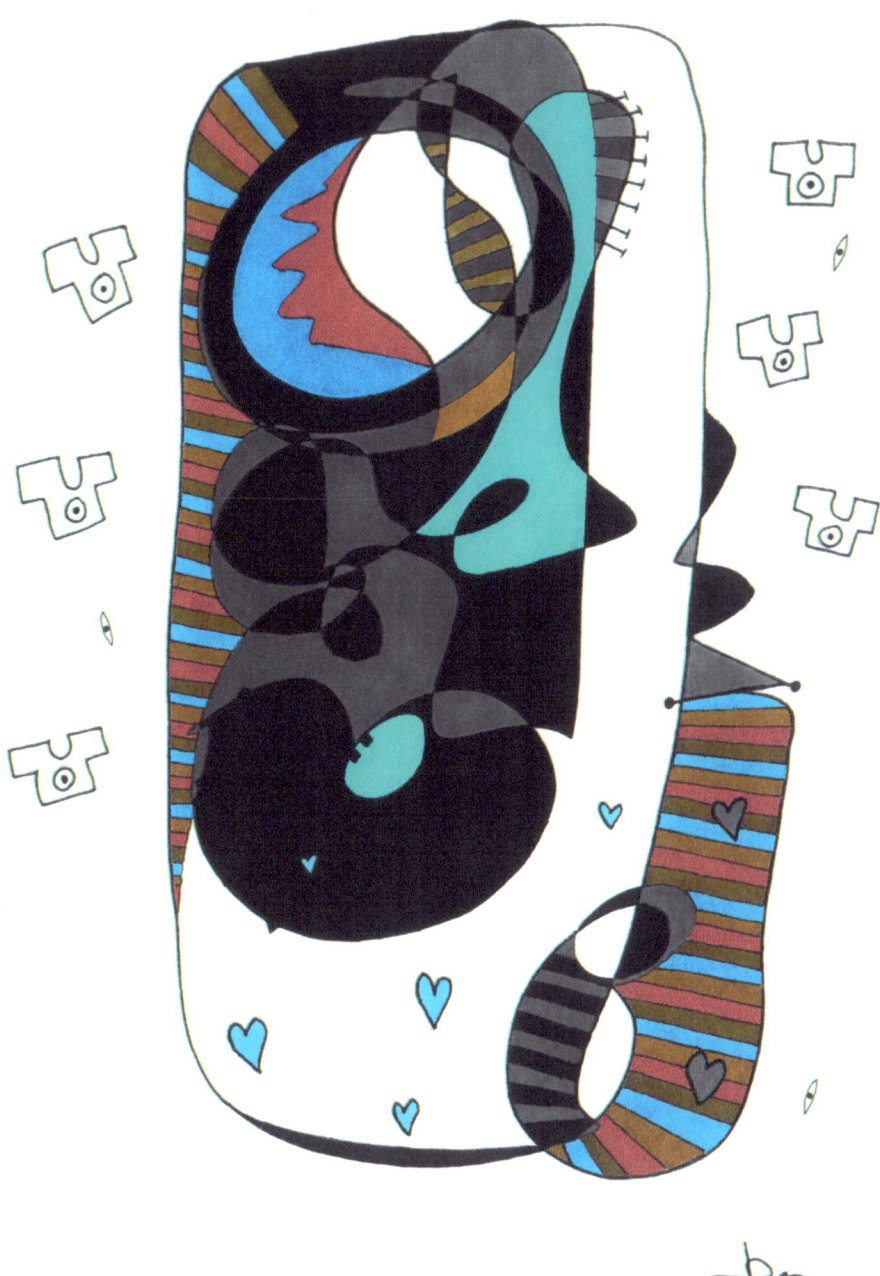

Ron.

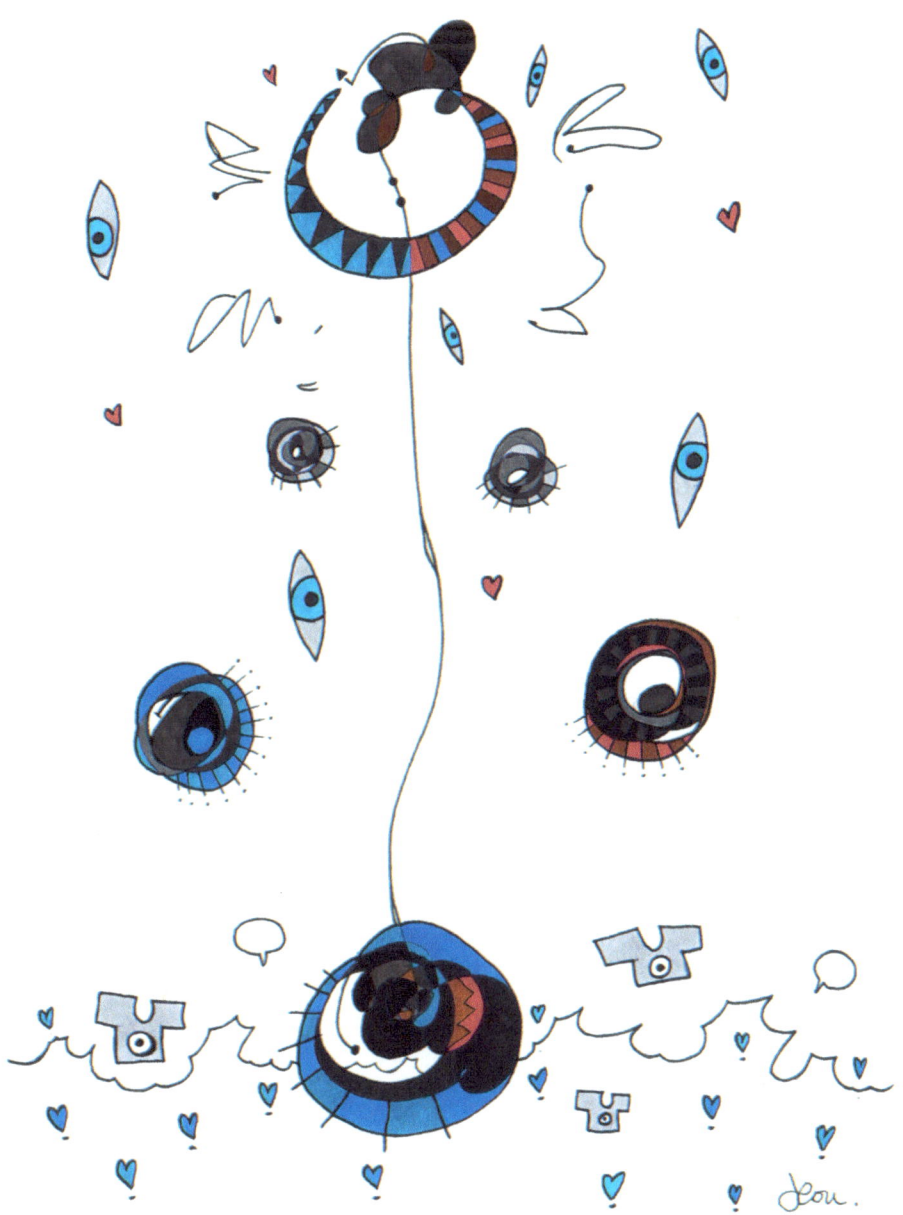

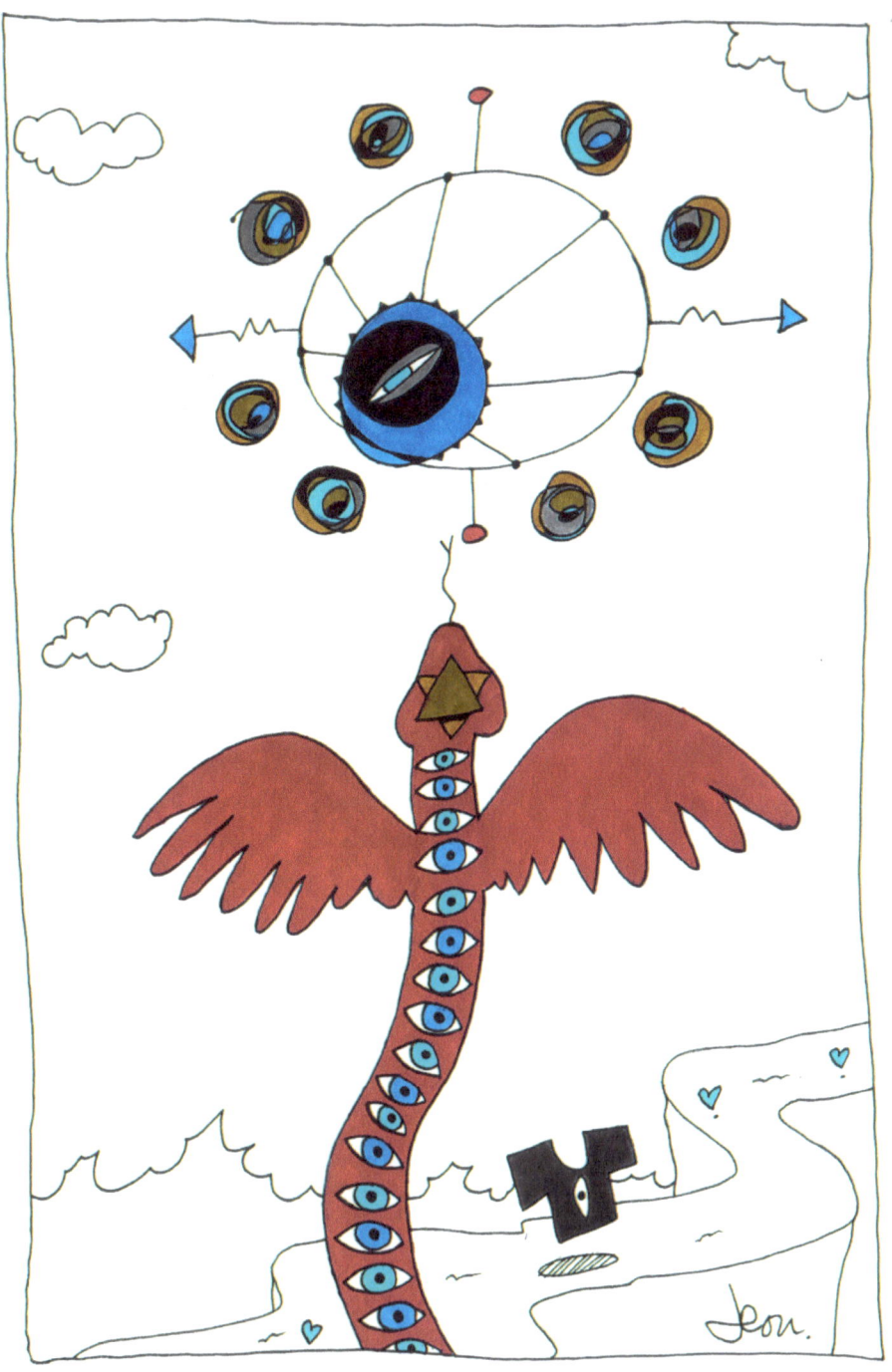

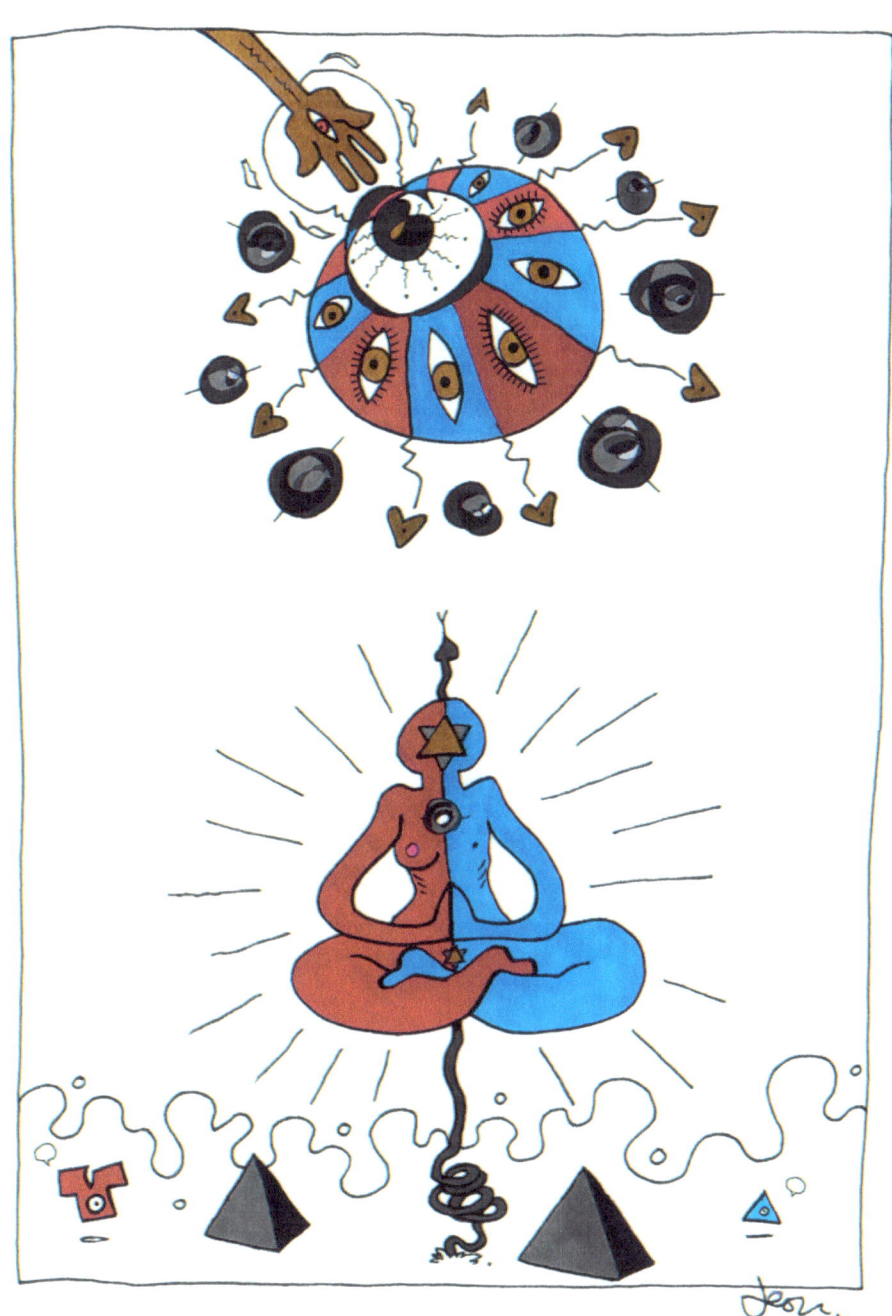

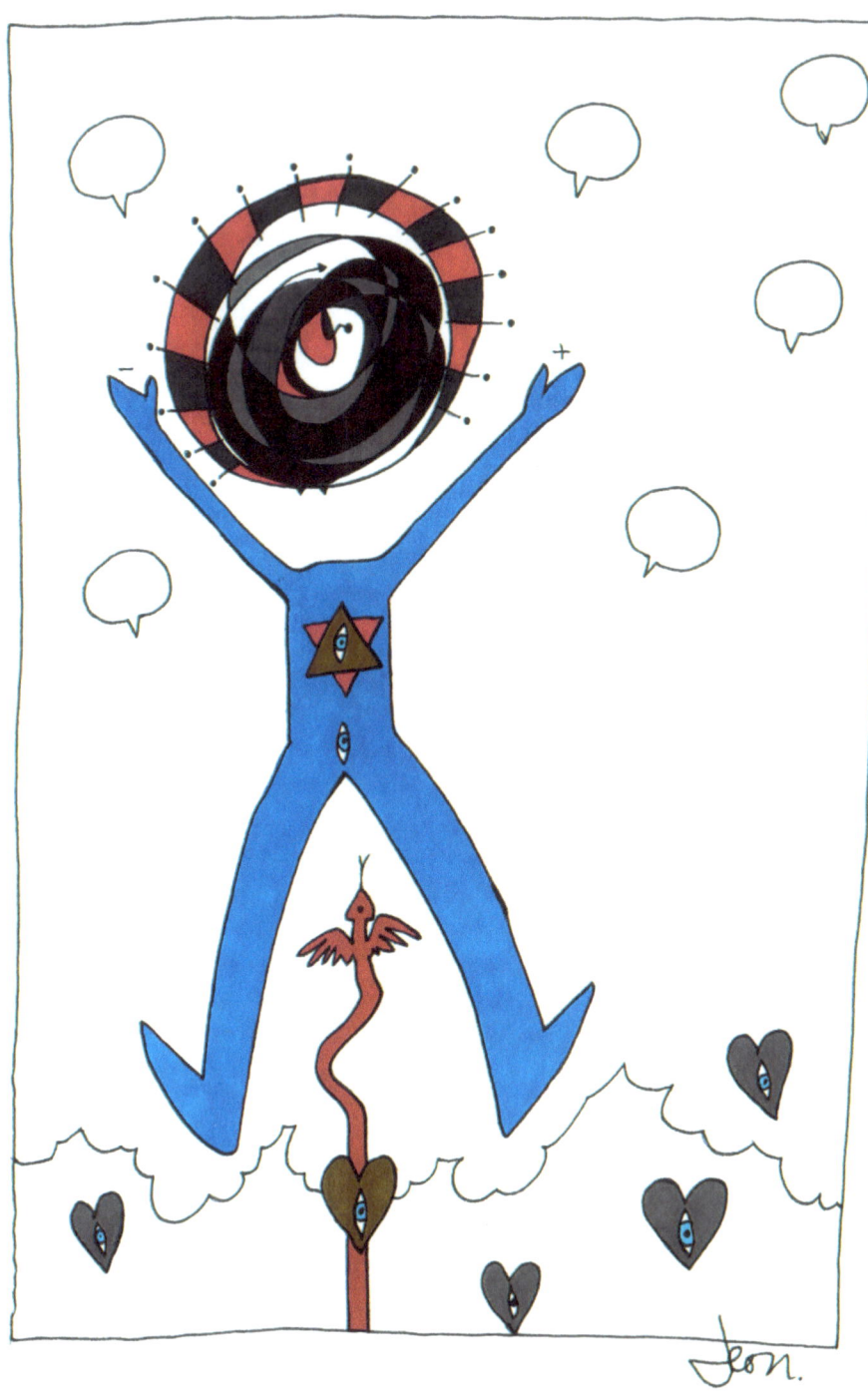

www.ingramcontent.com/pod-product-compliance
Lightning Source LLC
Chambersburg PA
CBHW041204180526
45172CB00006B/1188